Deconstructing Travel

Deconstructing Travel

Cultural Perspectives on Tourism

ARTHUR ASA BERGER

ALTAMIRA
PRESS

A Division of
ROWMAN & LITTLEFIELD PUBLISHERS, INC.
Walnut Creek • Lanham • New York • Toronto • Oxford

AltaMira Press
A division of Rowman & Littlefield Publishers, Inc.
1630 North Main Street, #367
Walnut Creek, California 94596
www.altamirapress.com

Rowman & Littlefield Publishers, Inc.
A wholly owned subsidiary of The Rowman & Littlefield Publishing Group, Inc.
4501 Forbes Boulevard, Suite 200
Lanham, Maryland 20706

PO Box 317
Oxford
OX2 9RU, UK

British Library Cataloguing in Publication Information Available

Library of Congress Cataloging-in-Publication Data

Berger, Arthur Asa, 1933–
  Deconstructing travel : cultural perspectives on tourism / Arthur Asa Berger.
    p. cm.
  Includes bibliographical references and index.
  ISBN 0-7591-0723-8 (hardcover : alk. paper) — ISBN 0-7591-0724-6
(pbk. : alk. paper)
    1. Tourism—Social aspects. I. Title.
  G155.A1B435 2004
  306.4'819—dc22

2004008563

Printed in the United States of America

♾™ The paper used in this publication meets the minimum requirements of American
National Standard for Information Sciences—Permanence of Paper for Printed Library
Materials, ANSI/NISO Z39.48–1992.

For my grandchildren Ariel and Seth

Contents

Self-contempt and a sense of fraudulence distinguish the attitude of contemporary self-conscious travelers. There is a touching desperation in the attempts of professional tourists, well-funded anthropologists, and recording travelers, to distinguish themselves from the traveling masses and run-of-the-mill adventurers. The most characteristic mark of the tourist is the wish to avoid tourists and places they congregate. But this is merely evidence of the fact that travel is no longer a means of achieving distinction. It is a way of achieving and realizing a norm, the common identity we all share—the identity of the stranger.

—*Eric J. Leed*, The Mind of the Traveler: From Gilgamesh to Global Tourism

Preface

When I was a young boy, by some curious circumstance, my family owned a book about Livingstone and Stanley's adventures in Africa, which I found absolutely fascinating and read many times. The book exposed me to a world that was far removed from mine, growing up in Boston. Boston billed itself, showing considerable hubris, as "the hub of the universe." Boston may have thought itself the hub of the universe, but my reading, which branched out as I got older to other adventurers in other lands, identified many other interesting places in the world that I thought I would like to visit some day.

I suspect that this childhood book played a large role in making me decide to travel. There was another influence as well. I took art classes Saturdays at the Museum of Fine Arts, and one of my teachers, Alma LeBrecht, was a real world traveler. I stayed at the museum all day long on Saturdays. During lunch, Alma LeBrecht talked about her various travels in India and other far-off lands. I took these classes in the late 1940s, when people didn't flit about the world the way they do now, and when a single woman traveling to exotic sites such as India and China was most unusual.

MY TRAVELS

Since my first trip to Europe at the age of 22, one way or another I've managed to travel to quite a number of places—all of the European countries and a number of others, such as Turkey, Lebanon, Israel, Brazil, China, Vietnam, Japan, Korea, Thailand, Malaysia, and Morocco. I was drafted and served in the army from 1956 to 1958. When I got out, I took "the grand tour," traveling around Europe for a year. After I got married and had a family, I received a Fulbright grant to Italy and lived for a year, in 1963, in Milan, where I taught American literature at the University of Milan. I also spent a year in London, ten years later, on sabbatical—doing research on English popular culture. In a number of cases my visits to foreign countries were connected to lectures I gave on various aspects of American popular culture and the media.

So, I've done some traveling—but not as much as many people I've met who, somehow, are always on the move and seem compelled to see as much of the world as possible. One of the ironic aspects of being a tourist, as Eric Leed's quotation at the beginning of this chapter points out, is that tourists seek to visit places of interest to tourists where there aren't other tourists. So there is a search to go to places before they have been "discovered." Some tourists seem driven. Business travelers often travel a great deal, but not for pleasure, so I don't consider them to be tourists. I will use the terms *travel* and *tourism* to represent traveling for pleasure and reserve *business travel* for when I'm talking about travel as part of work.

THE CULTURAL STUDIES APPROACH TO TOURISM

In recent decades, scholars in a variety of disciplines recognized that it was useful to study topics they were interested in from a multidisciplinary perspective. This is the case whether we're talking about specific texts (the term used in academic discourse for a particular film, advertisement, television show, novel, or any other work) or more general subjects such as tourism. This multidisciplinary approach informs "cultural studies," which uses insights from a number of different disciplines from the humanities and social sciences, to deal with topics being investigated.

Cultural criticism should be seen as an activity and not a discipline—an activity in which researchers can use literary and aesthetic theory, interpretive theories (such as semiotics, psychoanalytic, sociological, anthropological, and Marxist), and any other means and methods they can find that help make sense of various aspects of contemporary (and not so contemporary) culture and society.

The cultural studies movement developed out of work done at the University of Birmingham's Centre for Contemporary Cultural Studies, which started publishing a journal, *Working Papers in Cultural Studies*, in 1971. It dealt with media, popular culture, subcultures, gender issues, ideological issues, race, social movements, and everyday life, among other things. Although the journal did not last very long, it had an important impact on the way scholars conducted research on media and culture.

Let me offer an image that will help explain why cultural studies make sense. Imagine that six scholars, each representing a different academic discipline, are standing in a circle around a statue. Each scholar sees part of the statue but not all of it; thus, what he or she says about it from this particular perspective may be correct, but it doesn't tell the whole story. To see all of the sculpture, the scholars need to walk around it, and even then they still are limited to what they can see, at any given moment, from their particular points of view. The problems scholars working in cultural studies face involve finding ways to integrate the different disciplinary perspectives and means of interpretation they use in a meaningful way.

John Godfrey Saxe's famous poem "The Blind Men and the Elephant" is relevant to this discussion. In this poem, several blind men of Indostan each touch different parts of the elephant. Each of the blind men who touch its different parts (tusks, tail, sides, ears, legs, and trunk) offer conflicting descriptions of what an elephant is really like. The last verse in this poem is to the point:

> And so these men of Indostan
> Disputed loud and long,
> Each in his own opinion
> Exceeding stiff and strong,
> Though each was partly in the right,
> And all were in the wrong.

The cultural studies approach to tourism tries to avoid being partially right but generally in the wrong by looking at tourism from a number of different disciplinary perspectives—to gain insights that a single disciplinary approach cannot offer.

Tourism can be seen, then, as a cultural phenomenon that is too large and too complicated—possessing social, cultural, psychological, economic, political, and other dimensions—for any one discipline to deal with adequately.

WHAT THIS BOOK DEALS WITH

Deconstructing Travel examines tourism as a cultural phenomenon and attempts to understand why tourism has become the biggest industry in the world. If you sit in the international lounge of a major airport, you see people in all kinds of different dress. People are traveling all over the world all the time. Who are these people? Where are they from? Where are they going? Why are they traveling? I answer these and many other questions related to tourism and travel in this book.

Thus, in the first chapter, "Travelers and Tourists," you will find a discussion of my suggestion, found in my "myth model," that tourism can be understood as a modern manifestation of ancient mythic beliefs. I also deal with ideological interpretations of myth and discuss the work of the semiotician Roland Barthes, who has some fascinating things to say about tourism in his books on French culture (*Mythologies*) and Japanese culture (*Empire of Signs*). In addition, I consider the way tourism and travel can be defined and the relationship between tourism and consumer cultures. I discuss the work of political scientist Aaron Wildavsky and social anthropologist Mary Douglas, who argue that the choices people make about where and how to travel are socially determined, by the consumer culture to which they belong, rather than being a matter of individual psychology. I also discuss the relationship between explorers, settlers, travelers, and tourists.

In "Aspects of Travel and Tourism," the second chapter, I deal with some of the ideas of postmodern thinkers as they relate to tourism and also consider some of the more traditional topics generally dealt with in studies of tourism: the tourist "gaze," the search tourists make for authenticity and the exotic, the relationship between tourism and pilgrimages, the notion that travel is a rite of passage, and the role of travel agents and others in the travel industry.

My third chapter, "The Uses of Travel and Tourism," applies the "uses and gratifications methodology" (originally used to determine why people watch certain television programs and listen to certain radio shows) to tourism. I also consider demographic matters relating to tourism such as the gender, age, and socioeconomic status of tourists. I conclude the chapter by dealing with travelers as risk takers and as strangers (in strange lands) plus allied matters including tourism and the nostalgia for the past, and travel as a means of personal transformation.

Tourism is an enormous industry, and so it is only logical that I would deal with economic factors relating to tourism in the fourth chapter of this book, "The Tourism Industry." I discuss topics such as the size of the tourism industry, the most popular destinations for tourists, the different kinds of tourists, the countries whose populations travel the most, the changes that have taken place in the tourism industry over the years, and the impact of historical events on the tourism industry.

In chapter 5, "Travel Advertising: Images and Language," I deal with travel advertising—with the images ones sees in print advertisements and television commercials and with the language found in advertisements. I also analyze one randomly chosen issue of a popular tourism magazine, *Travel + Leisure*, to see what its advertisements reveal about tourism. I consider, for example, the appeals made in travel advertising and the way language is used to stimulate desire in those exposed to travel advertising in all media.

Chapter 6, "Travel Writing as an Art Form," discusses some of the conventions found in travel writing and literary methods used by travel writers. The best travel writers are, I suggest, amateur cultural anthropologists who not only describe their activities in their travels but also reveal a good deal about the cultures and societies they are visiting. I also discuss the work of Claude Lévi-Strauss, probably the most influential anthropologist of recent years. He wrote an important book on Brazil, *Tristes Tropiques*, and, it turns out, is a marvelous travel writer, though he says he hates travel writing.

In chapter 7, "The Impact of Tourism," I deal with the cultural imperialism hypothesis and its critique of tourism and with the related matter of tourism as a global phenomenon. I cover a number of topics here, such as the role of tourism in the destruction, and in some cases preservation, of nature and the way tourism has affected "old town" sections of some cities. I also consider the changes that have taken place in museums and the importance of other elite cultural institutions for tourism.

In chapter 8, "Disneyland and Walt Disney World," I analyze the significance of two of the most important tourist destinations and consider what these tourist sites reflect about contemporary American culture and society. I offer a critique of Disneyland by a psychiatrist, who deals with Disney's psychological makeup and how that has affected Disneyland and Walt Disney World. I also consider postmodernist and other critiques of these parks.

Finally, in chapter 9, "The End of the Road," I offer some concluding thoughts on tourism's global impact and the psychological value of travel. Unless we refuse to ever leave our hometowns or the cities where we were born and grew up, sooner or later we all become tourists. I suggest that travel can be seen as a kind of narrative that we write about ourselves—if not in books and journals that we keep, then in our minds.

In actuality, tourism is not only the largest industry in the world but also a subject that touches on an almost endless number of things in people's lives.

This means that trying to explain tourism's importance—its social, economic, cultural, and psychological significance—is an extremely difficult task. We must learn how to deal with all aspects of the tourism phenomenon, more or less at the same time.

I would hope that by reading this book you will gain insights—that a cultural studies approach uniquely offers—into the role tourism and travel play in contemporary society and, by extension, since you've probably done a bit of traveling yourself, the role travel has played in your life.

Acknowledgments

I would like to thank my editor, Grace Ebron, for suggesting I write this book and for her endless patience and continuous encouragement as I worked on it. Mitch Allen, the president of AltaMira Press, ordered all his editors to "make Berger rewrite every book five times," and it turns out that I actually ended up rewriting and revising this book five times. This happens to be the fifth book I've published with AltaMira—which may explain why I was required to revise it five times. I hope that I won't be required to revise my tenth book with AltaMira ten times!

I was fortunate enough to receive some helpful suggestions from a number of scholars, whose names I do not know, and I wish to thank them for their help. I greatly benefited from their comments. Let me also express my appreciation to the staff of AltaMira and to everyone involved in the production of this book.

Deconstructing Travel

What gives value to travel is fear. It is the fact that, at a certain moment, when we are so far from our own country . . . we are seized by a vague fear, and this instinctive desire to go back to the protection of old habits. This is the most obvious benefit of travel. At that moment we are feverish but also porous, so that the slightest touch makes us quiver to the depths of our being. . . . This is why we should not say that we travel for pleasure. There is no pleasure in travelling, and I look upon it as an occasion for spiritual testing. Pleasure takes us away from ourselves the same way that distraction, as in Pascal's use of the world, takes us away from God. Travel, which is like a greater and grave science, brings us back to ourselves.

—*Albert Camus*, Notebooks, 1935–1942

1

Travelers and Tourists

For as long as human beings have been on the face of the earth, they have moved from place to place—for any one of a number of different reasons. We know, from archaeological investigations, that there have been incredible migrations of our ancient ancestors over the millennia. And nowadays people continue to travel all over the world. Why they travel and what it all means is the subject of this book.

TRAVELERS IN THE BIBLE AND IN MYTHOLOGY

The Old Testament is, in one sense, a history of the travels of the Jews after they escaped from Egypt, wandering around for forty years before settling in what we now call Israel. Moses, who fled from Egypt and settled in Midian, described himself then, as many modern-day travelers might describe themselves now when they travel to foreign countries, as "a stranger in a strange land." Indeed, the history of the Jewish people is that of wanderers—after being thrown out of Spain and many other countries in the middle ages.

But Jews are not the only people who have been forced to wander around the world, and even today there are incredible migrations of peoples escaping war or famine, looking for work, and going on religious pilgrimages. A pilgrimage, as I define the term, involves people who travel to visit holy sites, such as Israel for Jews, Fatima and Lourdes for Roman Catholics, and Mecca for Muslims. I will discuss pilgrimages in more detail later in the book, but let me point out here that there is reason to suggest that all travel and tourism has a touch of the "sacred" to it.

It can be argued that a mythic dimension is present in all the trips we take, even if they don't have an overtly religious dimension to them. Students of mythology have suggested that there are often hidden and unrecognized

3

mythological roots to many of the things we do. Myths can be defined as sacred stories that, among other things, connect individuals with their cultures and with various activities that take place in their cultures.

In his book *Mythologies*, French semiotician Roland Barthes deals with myths and attendant mystifications and delusions that he finds in French culture. He defines myths essentially in ideological terms and devotes several chapters in his book to travel. The first, "The Writer on Holiday," deals with attitudes people have about writers on holiday:

> "Holidays" are a recent social phenomenon, whose mythological development, incidentally, would be interesting to trace. At first a part of the school world, they have become, since the advent of holidays with pay, a part of the proletarian world, or at least the world of working people. To assert that this phenomenon can henceforth concern writers, that the specialists of the human soul are also subjected to the common status of contemporary labour, is a way of convincing our bourgeois readers that they are indeed in step with the times. (1972, 29)

Ultimately, Barthes concludes, "the good-natured image of 'the writer on holiday' is therefore no more than one of those cunning mystifications which the Establishment practices to better enslave its writers."

Another chapter of *Mythologies* that deals with travel and tourism is "The 'Blue Blood' Cruise," which is about "the setting out to sea of a hundred or so royals on a Greek yacht, the *Agamemnon*." On this cruise, kings play at being ordinary men, and this leads Barthes to a disquisition on the nature of kingship:

> Kings are defined by the purity of their race (Blue Blood) like puppies, and the ship, the privileged locus of any "closure," is a kind of modern Ark where the main variations of the monarchic species are preserved. To such an extent that the chances of certain pairings are openly computed. Enclosed in their floating stud-farm, the thoroughbreds are sheltered from all mongrel marriages, all is prepared for them (annually, perhaps?) to be able to reproduce among themselves. (1972, 33)

The disdain Barthes has for these royals is evident in his language and the comparisons he makes; it is also interesting to see how he, too, ties this form of travel to the mythic—namely Jonah's ark—and to see how he points our attention to an important element of travel, namely the desire of people from certain social classes to maintain social distance from those not like themselves.

Barthes has also written a book completely devoted to travel—his *Empire of Signs*, written in 1970 and translated to English in 1982. In this book, which is similar in design to *Mythologies*, Barthes analyzes Japanese culture by discussing some of its most interesting commonplace objects and activities, or, in semiotic parlance, signs. Thus, he deals with topics such as Japanese chopsticks, Pachinko, bowing, haiku, and tempura. These all function as signifiers of important beliefs and myths found in Japanese culture and society.

As Barthes explains,

> The author has never, in any sense, photographed Japan. Rather, he has done the opposite: Japan has starred him with any number of "flashes"; or, better still, Japan has afforded him a situation of writing. (1970, 4)

In twenty-six short essays, then, Barthes attempts to capture the essence of Japanese culture and offers us an unusual kind of travel book, one that deals with the hidden codes and unique practices that make Japan such a distinctive and fascinating country.

Mircea Eliade is another scholar who has written extensively on the subject of myths. He describes myths as sacred histories and suggests in *The Sacred and the Profane* that myths are "the paradigmatic model for all human activities" (1961, 97–98). He also has written that "the modern man who feels and claims that he is nonreligious still retains a large stock of camouflaged myths and degenerated rituals" (1961, 204–205). Eliade offers examples such as New Year's Eve parties, parties given when one is promoted, and battles between monsters and heroes in films.

THE MYTH MODEL

If myths are a paradigmatic model for all human behavior, as Eliade asserts, we can expect to see myths informing our daily activities, even though we may not be aware that this is the case. I have developed what I call a "myth model" and suggest that we can also find certain myths informing psychoanalytic theory (think, for example, of the Oedipus myth and the Oedipus complex) and can trace these myths in historical experiences, in elite literature, in popular culture, and in everyday life.

Let me offer an example of how myth pervades these phenomenon in my myth model. I will deal with the mythological hero Odysseus—also known as Ulysses—as the paradigmatic tourist, the UR traveler, the model for all travelers, even though most of us don't take such extended or exciting trips.

Myth	Odysseus goes to Troy, spends ten years there fighting in the Trojan war, then returns on a voyage that takes another ten years and is full of hazards and dangers.
Psychoanalytic Concept	Wanderlust—the need some people have to travel endlessly, searching, some theorists suggest, for an idealized perfect father or mother figure.
Historical Events	De Tocqueville travels to America and later writes a book, *Democracy in America.*
Elite Culture	Thomas Mann's "Death in Venice" Jonathan Swift's *Gulliver's Travels*
Everyday Life	A person takes a tour to Turkey and visits Troy.
Popular Culture	Travel magazines, television travel shows, and travel guidebooks about Turkey and Troy

This little exercise suggests that mythological foundations that become removed from their sacred origins may be behind many of the things we do. In the case of my model, this involves travel to Turkey and a visit to see the remnants of Troy, but we can apply the myth model to many things we do.

My point is that many of our activities are what Eliade described earlier as camouflaged myths and rituals, and one of the most important of those camouflaged myths and rituals involves travel. Note, also, that Odysseus faced dangers in his travels—dangers that heightened the significance of his voyage just as interruptions, disruptions, and a certain element of anxiety about one's safety heighten the experience of travel for many tourists.

The question arises then—what is travel? What does it mean to travel?

WHAT IS TRAVEL?

"Travel," a wiseguy once said, "is what travelers do. And what do travelers do? Travel!" This is, obviously, a circular argument that has "movement," we might say, but doesn't get us anywhere. For our purposes, touristic travel involves people going somewhere from somewhere else, generally to a place that is distant, and then returning. When we commute from our houses to our jobs we are, literally speaking, traveling, but not in the sense that I am using the term in this book, which involves a break in our everyday routines and movement to distant places, for short periods of time, and then a return to one's starting point. Touristic traveling, as I interpret the term, is a leisure time experience; its goal is pleasure, entertainment, and education.

Many people who do a great deal of traveling don't fit under this definition. For example, business travel involves movement from place to place—but essentially to conduct business. Many members of the U.S. armed forces do a great deal of traveling—to fight wars and to man military outposts all over the world. But this also can be seen as a kind of business travel. Sometimes businessmen and soldiers have time to be tourists and visit cathedrals, temples, museums, and other places of interest, which means they are able to mix tourism with business travel.

Travel is associated with an adventurous personality, with independence, and with curiosity. The Camus quote at the beginning of the chapter alludes to the fact that travelers frequently must deal with delays of one sort or another, often make changes in their plans, and sometimes even face danger—all of which heighten their feelings of adequacy and of being alive. There is always an element of physical discomfort and sometimes even pain connected with international travel; travelers often become very tired from the long flights necessary to travel great distances and often suffer from jet lag. Being a tourist is hard work, as every traveler knows.

Some people describe themselves as travelers and not tourists, perhaps because the connotations of *tourist* are not positive. Travel suggests effort while tourism suggests ease. But what about adventure tours, which can be quite strenuous? Even many ordinary tours, because of their rapid pace and all the sightseeing involved, are also fairly arduous. So is there a difference between being a traveler and a tourist? Not as I use the terms. People travel to foreign lands, and some of these travelers may take organized tours, of one sort or another.

TOURISTS

At the root of this term is the Greek word *tornos*, which is a primitive tool for making a circle. A tour, as it is conventionally used in the travel industry, is a group form of travel that generally has the following characteristics: the route is very specific; one moves from point to point or city to city rather quickly ("If it's Wednesday, this must be Lisbon"); a certain element of regimentation is involved ("Will everyone please get on the bus!"); and eventually one returns to where one started.

But no universally accepted definition of tourism exists; different scholars define it in different ways. The World Tourism Organization defines tourism as follows:

> It comprises the activities of persons traveling to and staying in places outside their usual environment for not more than one consecutive year for leisure, business and other purposes not related to the exercise of an activity remunerated from within the place visited. (www.world-tourism.org/statistics/tsa_project/TSA_in_depth/chapters/ch3-1.htm [accessed May 15, 2002])

This definition is too broad, as far as I'm concerned, and I will offer some details that will provide more insights into what tourism is and isn't. For many people, as I suggested earlier, the term *tourism* has negative connotations because of the supposed superficiality and regimentation of some package tours and because of the connection of tourism with consumer culture.

Let me offer another definition of the term *tourist*. In his book *The Tourist: A New Theory of the Leisure Class*, Dean MacCannell defines the tourist as follows:

> "Tourist" is used to mean two things in this book. It designates actual tourists: sightseers, mainly middle-class, who are at this moment deployed through the entire world in search of experience. I want the book to serve as a sociological study of this group. But I should make it known that, from the beginning, I intended something more. The tourist is an actual person, or real people are actually tourists. At the same time, "the tourist" is one of the best models for modern-man-in-general. I am equally interested in "the tourist" in this second, metasociological sense of the term. Our first apprehension of modern civilization, it seems to me, emerges in the mind of the tourist. (1976, 1)

For MacCannell, then, tourists are middle-class (mainly) sightseers in quest of experience who also serve as models or prototypes for modern man. This would suggest, if you push this notion to its logical conclusion, that to be a human, or, at least, modern man (and woman), is to be a tourist. *Homo sapiens* has been re placed by homo tornos.

TOURISTS AND TRAVELERS

There is the question of whether important differences exist between tourists, travelers, visitors, and excursionists. Visitors are generally defined as people who spend time in a foreign country. But how long must a person stay in a distant place to stop being considered a visitor? And how do we, or can we, differentiate visiting from traveling and touring? Excursionists are people who spend a short time at a site—such as those who take a day trip to a different city or visit a city or place of interest while on a tour. Travelers go places and then come back . . . but so do tourists.

So, what is a tourist? What is tourism? International tourism, the kind of tourism I deal with primarily in this book, is generally understood to have the following characteristics:

It is *temporary*, for a relatively short period of time.

It is *voluntary*, done by choice.

It is done in *foreign* lands.

It is tied to *leisure* and *pleasure* and *consumer culture*.

It is *discretionary*, done because the tourist desires to do so.

It is done for *pleasure, entertainment*, and related considerations.

It is *not involved with business* and earning money while abroad.

It is based on a *round trip*, tied to a return to one's point of origin.

It is made possible by *technological developments* in travel and communication, among other things.

It is a *mass phenomenon*, done by large numbers of people.

But what do we say about a business traveler in Düsseldorf who takes a couple of hours to go to Cologne to look at the great cathedral there? Do we not have here a mixture of travel and tourism? Or what about a tourist who meets with someone, for a short period of time, about a business matter during a visit to a foreign land. Does a short period of time devoted to business make a tourist a business traveler? If you live in San Diego and were to drive to Ensenada, Mexico, for lunch and then come back, were you a tourist or a traveler?

It is obvious, then, that it is frequently very difficult to differentiate between travel and tourism, except, perhaps, in their most extreme forms. The difference between the two has historical roots. A hundred years ago, travel was more or less reserved for the elite; when mass transportation means developed—railroads, airplanes, cruise ships—travel then became available to the masses. This kind of travel, when linked with the phenomena described earlier, is now often described as tourism.

So defining tourism is, to a large degree, based on the mind-set and ideological belief system of the person labeling some people as tourists and others as travelers. Some might say that a traveler is someone who goes places and a tourist is someone who sees places, but that distinction seems a bit forced because when travelers get to wherever they are going, they generally like to look around and see the sights as well. And tourists have to travel to get where they want to go. So I consider the terms to be synonymous, generally speaking, especially when they relate to distant or overseas travel.

EXPLORERS, SETTLERS, TRAVELERS, AND TOURISTS

Perhaps it is possible to differentiate between travelers and tourists in a different way—over time. I offer here a short hypothetical analysis of the relationship that might exist among explorers, settlers, travelers, and tourists, based on the American experience. Explorers can be understood as people who venture into lands where few others have gone, mapping the territory and interacting with native peoples—if there are any. Explorers do not know what they will find, and an element of adventure and danger is often connected to exploration.

In the early days of America, explorers ventured into a great wilderness, what we called "the frontier." Once the explorers returned with stories about their adventures, others came who settled America and brought "civilization." Then, after the settlers came travelers and eventually mass tourism.

Of course some explorers go to seldom-visited "unknown" lands that are already settled, lands that may have highly developed cultures and social institutions but are not on the touristic map, so to speak. The information these explorers provide about these lands brings travelers, and the information travelers provide often leads to large numbers of people visiting a given place—that is, to mass tourism.

Tourism is a mass phenomenon in that huge numbers of people now travel and visit near or distant parts of their own countries or other lands. It is also very complex because it requires a number of institutions to sustain itself— what we might call a touristic infrastructure: travel agents, hotels and inns, museums, sports arenas, restaurants, entertainment sites, natural beauty sites, guides, transportation facilities, and so on. Tourism is the largest industry in the world, which, some theorists have argued, has been turned in recent years into a gigantic collection of tourist sites of varying natures to suit the inclinations of different kinds of tourists.

TRIPS AND VACATIONS

Tourists take trips. That is, they go places either independently or with others on tours or cruises or expeditions. They generally go to certain places of touristic interest, what I call tourist meccas, for specific periods of time, at the end of which they return home. People who are retired and who like to travel can take trips whenever they want, but those who aren't retired must fit their trips into their vacation periods. Since Americans, as a rule, have shorter vacations than do Europeans, the trips Americans take need to be planned carefully. We must keep in mind that many workers in Europe have six weeks of vacation compared with two or three weeks for the typical American worker, many of whom don't take any vacations at all.

Here are some statistics of interest about workers in the United States (all figures are approximate, taken from various sources) relative to vacations and tourism:

Sixteen percent of American workers say they are too busy to take off all the vacation days that are due to them.

Twenty percent of American workers never take vacations.

The average vacation time in the United States is thirteen days, compared with forty-two days in Europe.

Thirty-three percent of American workers check in with their bosses during vacations.

Forty percent of American workers skip summer vacations because of increased workloads and tighter budgets.

We see, then, that Americans (and I will use this term in this book to mean people from the United States) are very hard-working people who don't, as a rule, have the amount of free time that workers in European countries have, and in many cases are too busy to take vacations.

Although Americans usually don't have as much time off from their jobs as Europeans, some manage to do a great deal of traveling because some jobs, such as teaching, provide a lot of free time. And many Americans with only two weeks of vacation time often find ways to squeeze in trips longer than two weeks, using sick leave and taking unpaid leaves for short periods of time.

On a per capita basis, residents of the United Kingdom are the great tourists of the world, followed closely by Germany, France, Japan, and the United States. Residents of the United States spend $60 billion a year on tourism, but since there are some 270 million Americans, it works out to around a modest $222 per person.

At any given moment, large numbers of people are wandering around the world, functioning as tourists and travelers of one sort or another. I am talking about people on vacations, students who take time off from their studies to travel, workers who take sabbaticals (often without pay) to travel, students studying in foreign universities, elderly people taking tours, Australians with around-the-world air tickets (who often work in the U.K. for a year or two), backpackers seeing the world on the cheap, and so on. They all want to visit the interesting places of the world and often find themselves in tourist meccas.

TOURIST MECCAS

Tourist meccas, as I will use the term, are choice places for tourists to visit because of the beauty of the scenery, the richness of the culture, or certain events that may be taking place (carnivals, sporting events). The term *mecca* comes from Mecca, the city in Saudi Arabia that millions of Muslims visit each year on a religious pilgrimage. Tourist meccas can be cities, such as Paris, London, Florence, or San Francisco; they can be areas of a country, such as Normandy in France, Cappadocia in Turkey, the Greek Islands, or the Pacific Northwest in the United States; they can be villages or small cities that hold special interest, such as Lourdes in France or Perugia in Italy.

In all cases, tourist meccas offer something that attracts tourists, for one reason or another. It could be any number of factors, such as spectacular scenery or great museums. Perhaps the place has religious significance, or it is a center of gay and lesbian or heterosexual sex. Or maybe the location is simply pleasant and inexpensive. Some are standard tourist destinations and others are places that have been newly "discovered." The game for many travelers is to find undiscovered gems and visit them before mass tourism begins and they become overdeveloped meccas full of tourist traps.

The advent of mass tourism to a city or a place is a two-edged sword. On the one hand, tourists spend money on hotels, restaurants, transportation, and entertainment and generally do a good deal of shopping. This leads to new jobs and more money for the community as a whole, though much of this money has to be devoted to upgrading the infrastructure and taking care of the needs and wishes of tourists.

Tourism often leads to an increase in the cost of living for natives and, in some cases, to the displacement of locals, who, for example, may lose the easy access to beaches they had before beachfront hotels started springing up. Tourism often leads to the development of the sex industry and to various kinds of culture clashes between tourists and natives. Places that become tourist destinations become dependent on tourism, which becomes the tail that wags the dog. The place, the area, and often the entire country become extremely dependent on tourism, and attracting and satisfying tourists starts becoming a dominant aspect of economic planning and social life.

TOURISTS AS CONSUMERS

As I suggested earlier, tourism—now a global phenomenon—is the locus of a huge number of businesses connected to the movement of people from one place to another and of taking care of their many needs. I am talking about everything from taking cabs and buses to and from airports; booking airplane travel; staying in hotels and inns; dining in restaurants; shopping for souvenirs, gifts, and other items; visiting museums; going to concerts, operas, shows, and sporting events; finding sexual partners; and taking day tours and excursions.

In some cases, travelers stay at hotels booked by their tours. Their daily expenses are taken up by the tour companies. They have paid, up-front, for their hotels, transportation, and many if not all of their meals. In other cases, independent travelers spend money on the go, so to speak, for these matters.

We see, then, that a trip or a tour is just the tip of a huge iceberg involving many different institutions, organizations, and companies connected to the tourism industry. One way or another—in payments up-front to tour companies or cruise lines or in payments at each step of the process—money is continually changing hands.

What tourists are buying, primarily, are experiences—ones that they believe will educate them in terms of the ways other people live, elevate them spiritually, enhance their enjoyment of life, and, in the broadest sense possible, educate and entertain them. This is done by visiting, for varying lengths of time, other countries to get a sense of how people in these places live, what they have done in the past (their architecture, monuments, and historically interesting buildings), what kinds of things they eat, and how they amuse themselves, among other things.

Paul Fussell explains this link between tourism and education in his book *The Norton Book of Travel.* He writes that travel

> conveys the pleasure of learning new things, and as Aristotle observed over 2,300 years ago, not only philosophers but people in general like learning things, even if the learning comes disguised as "entertainment." It is as learners that explorers, tourists, and genuine travelers, otherwise so different in motives and behavior, come together. Explorers learn the contours of undiscovered shorelines and mountains, tourists learn exchange rates and where to go in Paris for the best hamburgers. . . . Travelers learn not just foreign customs and curious cuisines and unfamiliar beliefs and novel forms of government. They learn, if they are lucky, humility. Experiencing on their senses a world different from their own, they realize their provincialism and recognize their ignorance. (1987, 13–14)

The ultimate lesson we learn from our travels abroad, Fussell suggests, is humility, as we discover that people in other countries may have beautiful cities full of wonderful buildings and great museums. People in other lands also may drink better coffee and have tastier food than we do in America.

One thing that people search for when they travel abroad is different reference points and different ways of doing things from their everyday lives. We only make sense of things by seeing how they differ from other things. Swiss semiotician Ferdinand de Saussure explained that concepts have no meaning in themselves but only obtain meaning by being different from their opposites:

Language is a system of interdependent terms in which the value of each term results solely from the simultaneous presence of the others. . . . It is understood that . . . *concepts are purely differential and defined not by their positive content but negatively by their relations with the other terms of the system. Their most precise characteristic is in being what the others are not.* . . . Signs function, then, not through their intrinsic value but through their relative position. (1966, 114, 117–118) [My italics.]

The most important relationship for Saussure is opposition, "*being what the others are not.*" [My italics.] We make sense of things, in our everyday lives, by putting everything into a set of relationships and determining what something is by seeing what it isn't.

The same applies to cultures; we travel to experience differences, ranging from countries that are mildly different from the United States (Canada) to countries that are very different from the United States (Thailand, Bali, India), which we define as exotic. In a sense, we go traveling because we want to find out more about other countries; as Americans, we do this by seeing how other countries differ from the United States. We also travel for other reasons, such as to meet people in other lands and in so doing to discover our common humanity, to see beautiful sites, and to visit great buildings and see works of art in great museums.

Travel is based on a powerful desire to participate in history—to see where great events took place, to see where great writers and artists and scientists lived and to see how they lived, to experience the best that the world can offer us. So, we expect to get a great deal for our money, and many people feel that their travels and tours were worth the expense. Even people who have not been satisfied, for one reason or another, with their travel arrangements and with what happened on their travels and tours tend to convince themselves that their travels were worth the expense. Otherwise they would have to admit to themselves that they made a mistake in booking a tour with this or that company and going to the country they visited rather than someplace else.

THE CONSUMPTION IMPERATIVE

Another factor related to tourism as consumption is of interest. According to French sociologist Jean Baudrillard, there is an element of *compulsion* in tourism and all forms of consumption. Baudrillard explains that nowadays consumption must not be seen as a pleasure or a means of enjoyment but as a *duty*. In a fascinating reversal of the Puritan ethic of hard work, now enjoyment and consumption are the required "business" of the typical person who is, so to speak, forced to have fun:

> There is no question for the consumer, for the modern citizen, of evading this enforced happiness and enjoyment, which is the equivalent in the new ethics of the traditional imperative to labour and produce. Modern man spends less and less of his life in production within work and more and more of it in the *production* and continual innovation of his own needs and well-being. He must constantly see to it that all his potentialities, all his consumer capacities are mobilized. If he forgets to do so, he will be gently and insistently reminded that he has no right not to be happy. It is not, then, true that he is passive. He is engaged in—has to engage in— continual activity. . . . Hence the revival of a *universal curiosity*. . . . You have to try *everything*, for consumerist man is haunted by the fear of "missing" something, some form of enjoyment. You never know whether a particular encounter, a particular experience (Christmas in the Canaries, eel in whiskey, the Prado, LSD, Japanese-style love-making) will not elicit some "sensation." It is no longer desire, or even "taste," or a specific inclination that are at stake, but a generalized curiosity, driven by a vague sense of unease—it is the "fun morality" or the imperative to enjoy oneself, to exploit to the full one's potential for thrills, pleasure or gratification. (1998, 80)

Notice how travel and experiences of the differences found in various cultures play a part in Baudrillard's analysis.

Christmas in the Canaries is a somewhat exotic location that might help a consumer get the pleasures that are due him; conversely, she can go to Madrid and visit the Prado, satisfying her need for culture and refinement in one of the great museums of the world. Japanese-style love-making, whatever that may be, can be procured anywhere, but one must assume our consumer–tourist seeks as much authenticity as possible and goes to Japan to find the "real" thing. There is a driven aspect to all this, as if people, as consumers, feel they *must* suck the marrow out of life, and as tourists, see everything that is worth seeing and go every place that is worth visiting and eat everything that is worth eating.

The role of what we learn about foreign cultures and our imaginations envisioning them as "others" and, in extreme cases, "exotic," must be kept in mind. Long before we go abroad to visit new lands, we become virtual tourists who imagine what the places we will visit will be like, based on what we've seen in advertisements and on television documentaries and read in maga-zines, newspapers, and guidebooks. Baudrillard argues, in a different work, that there is no such thing as the "real" thing (aside, let me suggest, from Coca-Cola) and we all live in a world of simulations, but I must reserve this discussion for another part of my book.

What follows is an analysis suggesting that the concept of a "consumption culture" is inadequate, for it has been asserted by certain scholars that four—and no more than four—different consumption cultures or lifestyles in any society shape our decision making.

CONSUMER CULTURES AND TOURISM PREFERENCES

Tourism is often linked with consumer culture as an example of the importance of consumption in modern society and of consumption's global significance. But saying that such a thing as consumer culture exists is, it has been suggested, a bit of an oversimplification. There are, some scholars argue, not one but four different consumer cultures found in all societies, and these consumer cultures (or for certain purposes, called political cultures or lifestyles) are based on certain beliefs and values that members of each consumer culture hold in common.

My analysis draws on the work of the late political scientist Aaron Wildavsky and the distinguished social anthropologist Mary Douglas, with whom he often collaborated. According to Wildavsky, cultural theory tries to help people answer two basic questions. One involves identity: *Who am I?* The other involves action: *What should I do?* In his article "A Cultural Theory of Preference Formation," Wildavsky notes the following:

> The question of identity may be answered by saying that individuals belong to a strong group, a collective that makes decisions binding on all members or that their ties to others are weak in that their choices bind only themselves. The question of action is answered by responding that the individual is subject to many or few prescriptions, a free spirit or tightly constrained. The strength or weakness of group boundaries and the numerous or few, varied or similar prescriptions binding or freeing individuals are the components of their culture. (Berger 1989, 25)

Wildavsky suggests that four political cultures (and in the economic realm, as Douglas argues, four consumer cultures) arise from the answers to these two questions—what Wildavsky calls hierarchical, individualist, egalitarian, and fatalistic cultures.

We can see how these cultures are formed out of the *strength and weakness of group boundaries* and the *numbers and kinds of rules* and prescription. As Wildavsky explains,

> Strong groups with numerous prescriptions that vary with social roles combine to form hierarchical collectivism. Strong groups whose members follow few prescriptions form an egalitarian culture, a shared life of voluntary consent without coercion or inequality. Competitive individualism joins few prescriptions with weak group boundaries, thereby encouraging ever new combinations. When groups are weak and prescriptions strong—so that decisions are made for them by people on the outside—the controlled culture is fatalistic. (Berger 1989, 25)

Over the years Wildavsky changed the names of some of his cultures, but the four I have listed give a good representation of his ideas. He sometimes used hierarchical elitists or just plain elitists instead of hierarchical collectivism because he thought that description was a bit confusing.

One important point he makes is that *only* four political cultures are possible in any democratic society. Wildavsky suggests that individuals make political decisions on the basis of their allegiance to whichever group they find themselves in and not on the basis of self-interest, since they generally don't know (and can't know) what is in their self-interest. Table 1.1 lists the four political/consumer cultures and their relationship to group boundaries and prescriptions.

I should point out that members of these four political/consumer cultures generally don't identify themselves as members of one of these groups and aren't aware of their existence. People possess certain values and belief systems that Wildavsky and Douglas identify as placing them in one of the four cultures.

Table 1.1.   The Four Consumer Cultures

Culture	Group Boundaries	Number of Prescriptions
Hierarchists	Strong	Numerous and varied
Egalitarians (Enclavists)	Strong	Few
Individualists	Weak	Few
Fatalists (Isolates)	Weak	Numerous and varied

Mary Douglas takes these four cultures, which for her purposes she also describes as lifestyles, and substitutes the term *isolates* for *fatalists* and *enclavists* for *egalitarians*. She suggests that it is their membership in one of the four consumer cultures or lifestyles—each of which is antagonistic or in conflict with the three others—that explains people's consumer choices.

People may not be able to articulate the beliefs and values that put them in one of the four consumer cultures, but they recognize that their values and beliefs aren't those of members of the other consumer cultures. Consumption, then, is primarily based on cultural alignments and hostilities and is not based on individual wants or desires. And tourist preferences, of course, are a kind of consumption.

Douglas explains how all of this works in the realm of consumption in her essay "In Defense of Shopping," in a book edited by Pasi Falk and Colin Campbell, *The Shopping Experience*:

> None of these four lifestyles (individualist, hierarchical, enclavist, isolated) is new to students of consumer behavior. What may be new and unacceptable is the point that these are the only four distinctive lifestyles to be taken into account, and the other point, that each is set up in competition with the others. Mutual hostility is the force that accounts for their stability. These four distinct lifestyles persist because they rest on incompatible organizational principles. Each culture is a way of organizing; each is predatory on the others for time and space and resources. It is hard for them to coexist peacefully, and yet they must, for the survival of each is the guarantee of the survival of the others. Hostility keeps them going. (1997, 19)

She offers this theory to counter the theories of consumption that come from a framework based on individualist psychology and argues that "*cultural alignment is the strongest predictor of preferences in a wide variety of fields*" (1997, 23). [My italics.]

This suggests an inherent logic behind the shopping that people do. Furthermore, as Douglas argues, it is shoppers, consumers, whatever you wish to call them, who ultimately dictate what will be sold. We can see this as we examine the households of people from different consumer cultures. People in the different consumer cultures may have similar incomes (except for the fatalists/isolates, who are at the bottom of the income ladder, generally speaking), but the way they organize their households and their patterns of consumption are shaped by their membership in one of the four consumer cultures.

Douglas concludes that the notion that shopping is the expression of individual wants is incorrect, for this notion doesn't take into account cultural bias. She points out in the conclusion to her essay:

> The idea of consumer sovereignty in economic theory will be honoured in market research because it will be abundantly clear that the shopper sets the trends, and that new technology and new prices are adjuncts to achieving the shopper's goal. The shopper is not expecting to develop a personal identity by choice of commodities; that would be too difficult. *Shopping is agonistic, a struggle to define not what one is but what one is not.* [My italics.] When we include not one cultural bias, but four, and when we allow that each is bringing critiques against the others, and when we see that the shopper is adopting postures of cultural defiance, then it all makes sense. (1997, 30)

If Douglas is correct, and there are four distinct and mutually antagonistic lifestyles—what I've called consumer cultures—then the various kinds and modes of travel would have to appeal to members of one consumer culture and not the others. It wouldn't be socioeconomic class and discretionary income that shape travel decisions, but lifestyles or membership in one of the four consumer cultures and, more precisely, the desire to avoid members of the other consumer cultures. Her statement that shopping is an attempt to define what one is not calls to mind Ferdinand de Saussure's linguistic work and his notions that concepts are defined by being different from other concepts, by being in opposition to other concepts.

This means that members of each of the four antagonistic but mutually dependent consumer cultures or lifestyles look for different things when they travel and become different kinds of tourists. Let me hypothesize how people in each of the different consumer cultures might travel, assuming Douglas is correct about lifestyles.

Elitists search for hierarchy and obtain it when they travel by choosing luxury cruises or other luxury forms of travel, where they assume they will find—because of the cost of the travel—people like themselves. Luxury tours and everything associated with this kind of travel help them maintain social distance from members of the other consumer cultures. Individualists, not wanting anyone to tell them what to do, will travel independently, booking their hotels and other aspects of their trips through their travel agents or on their own, using the Internet. They will avoid packaged tours and will rent cars when possible. Egalitarians (enclavists) will take tours that focus on cultural matters, nature preservation, and ecotourism, wanting to do all they can to preserve nature and to show their links with people everywhere; they will avoid the kinds of tourism liked by elitists and individualists. Fatalists (isolates), who are generally at the bottom of the financial totem pole and have few resources, will take trips by automobiles or buses or short excursions. One reason why certain travel experiences may not be pleasurable for some people is that, by chance, they made the wrong kind of travel arrangements and ended up with people from a different and therefore antagonistic consumer culture.

Wildavsky and Douglas force us to consider that if scholars are unaware of the importance of the different consumer cultures, their analyses of travel and tourism as a kind of consumption may be overly simplistic and inadequate. If we want to know why people choose to travel the way they do, according to Wildavsky and Douglas, we shouldn't probe their minds and psyches but find out to which consumer culture they belong, since it is cultural alignment that explains preferences in politics and tourism and all other forms of consumption, including shopping—which is one of the main things people do when they are tourists.

Modernity first appears to everyone as it did to Lévi-Strauss, as disorganized fragments, alienating, wasteful, violent, superficial, unplanned, unstable and inauthentic. On second examination, however, this appearance seems almost a mask, for beneath the disorderly exterior, modern society hides a firm resolve to establish itself on a worldwide base.

Modern values are transcending the old divisions between the Communist East and the Capitalist West and between the "developed" and "third" worlds. The progress of modernity ("modernization") depends on its very sense of instability and inauthenticity. For moderns, reality and authenticity are thought to be elsewhere: in other historical periods and other cultures, in purer, simpler lifestyles. In other words, the concerns of moderns for "naturalness," their nostalgia and their search for authenticity are not merely casual and somewhat decadent, though harmless, attachments to the souvenirs of destroyed cultures and dead epochs. They are also components of the conquering spirit of modernity—the grounds of its unifying consciousness.

The central thesis of this book holds the empirical and ideological expansion of modern society to be intimately linked in diverse ways to modern mass leisure, especially to international tourism and sightseeing.

—*Dean MacCannell*, The Tourist: A New Theory of the Leisure Class

Aspects of Travel and Tourism

In this chapter, I consider a number of different aspects of travel—everything from the problem of tourist traps and the matter of the search for authenticity in tourism to the tourist gaze and the relationship between postmodern theory and travel. The quotation by Dean MacCannell that begins this chapter suggests that tourism can be seen, in part, as an escape attempt by people—fleeing certain unpleasant aspects of modernity. Tourists, he argues, are searching for the authentic and for the real; they find them in cultures that have "other" ways of life, often with purer, simpler lifestyles that they find attractive.

However, when tourists visit foreign countries in search of the authentic and the real, they often find themselves susceptible to a variety of different scams and other ploys, designed to trick them and to separate them from their money, one way or another.

TOURIST TRAPS

Tourist traps, as I use the term, are restaurants, hotels, resorts, and other tourist venues that exploit tourists by providing ersatz experiences geared at stereotyped notions some tourists have of what an authentic experience abroad should be. The problem tourists face is that in places of high touristic interest, tourist traps proliferate and thus tourists are increasingly susceptible to falling victim to them.

The term *tourist trap* is interesting. Traps are devices used to catch animals, and the metaphor of the trapped animal applied to the tourist, who is free to do whatever he or she desires until trapped, is a compelling one. Tourist traps are designed specifically for tourists who don't realize that they are being taken; many of these traps are characterized by kitschy staged events seen by tourists, who assumed they were going to get something authentic and traditional and often don't realize that what they've seen is ersatz.

For example, sometimes when tourists are wandering around with their guides, they encounter natives who invite them into their homes for a cup of tea. After tea, the host, it turns out, often has something to sell, which then transforms what seemed to be an example of hospitality into a commercial encounter. In many cases what appears to be a spontaneous example of friendship and hospitality between peoples is spurious because it has been arranged for by travel agencies and guides. Tourists, when asked if they wish to purchase something, suddenly realize that the experience isn't what they thought it was.

When my wife and I were in Morocco, on the last night of our group tour—and it was a wonderful experience, by the way—we all were taken as a tour "highlight" to a huge field full of large tents where we ate a mediocre dinner and then saw a rather bizarre so-called traditional Moroccan "spectacle." It featured singers, men on horses racing across the field firing guns, and a few other acts.

The price for this event, for people who booked the experience on their own, was $50 per person—an enormous amount of money in Morocco and a great deal more than the experience was worth. That Moroccan night was, to my mind, an example of a real tourist trap, designed and priced for tourists. It was so bizarre that it actually ended up being somewhat amusing. But I wouldn't have been amused if I had paid $100 for the experience.

THE TOURIST GAZE: SCOPOPHILIA

Some tourism scholars have suggested that there has been a change in tourism and that tourists have moved away from seeking interactions with natives in foreign lands in favor of seeing sights and capturing them on video or in photographs. What we have here is a kind of scopophilia (*scopo* = seeing and *philia* = loving), or loving by looking, which suggests there is an implicit erotic and even sexual dimension to the tourist gaze.

This applies not only to landscapes and cityscapes of interest but, as feminist theorists have suggested in discussing male and female relations and the "male gaze," also to gazing longingly at members of the opposite sex in foreign lands, where the gaze is explicitly sexual. In actuality, sexual tourism is a significant component of the tourism industry in many countries, and easy access to exotic women (and, in some cases, men) is an important inducement for some tourists.

The tourist, according to adherents of gaze theories, becomes concerned primarily with visually arresting places and with photographing them. This description of tourism is the subject of debate by other scholars who argue it is reductionistic. In her article "The Ideal Village: Interactions through Tourism in Central Anatolia" (Abram et al.), Hazel Tucker discusses some commonly held notions about the tourist gaze. She writes about tourist experiences in Goreme, a Cappadocian village in central Turkey:

> Analyses of tourism and tourist culture have tended to work through a purely visual framework, responding to the perpetual visualization in tourism-related discourses. Indeed, Urry (1990) argues that tourism is all about gazing upon particular scenes that are different from those encountered in everyday life. Furthermore, this view of tourism has led Urry to the conclusion that since postmodernity is marked by "the proliferation of images and symbols" . . . tourism is coming home, since it is now possible "to *see* many of the typical objects of the tourist gaze . . . in one's own living room, at the flick of a switch." (1997, 107)

This notion, Tucker argues, while popular, is simplistic and neglects the fact that many tourists actively seek interactions with people in the countries they visit and are not just interested in seeing sights and photographing them, even though the "moon-like" landscape in Goreme and other towns near it is quite fantastic.

She continues with her discussion of the touristic gaze and suggests that tourists aren't the only ones who gaze:

> The power of the photographic gaze is evident both through the symbolic representations "captured" within the pictures and in the actual process of taking photographs. Here we return to the idea of Goreme's being a "living museum," through which the people of the village are gazed upon, appropriated and collected. When photographed, the villages of Goreme are rendered "objects" . . . in an existential sense, in which there is a constant battle to be subject or object in relation to the other. . . . However, whilst much has been written about the power gaze of tourists upon "others," the return gaze is not so often considered. (1997, 108)

Tucker argues that during her stay in Goreme, the power of the gaze was not all one-sided in favor of the tourists. She suggests that the people of Goreme gazed back at tourists and, because they were on their home territory and were in larger numbers than the tourists, often their gaze was more powerful than that of the tourists.

It is, I would argue, reductionistic to assume that tourism is essentially visual (i.e., sightseeing) and that the gaze of the tourist in a foreign land is not returned by the gaze of the native. There is a tourist gaze because tourists seek places that are different—in some cases exotic—and the visual aspects of tourism are important, but so are other components of tourism. Tourists may become excited by people dressed in native costumes and gaze at them, but the natives, as often as not, gaze back. Each may find the other visually arresting and interesting . . . even exotic.

In this respect I can remember a relevant experience I had in China. My wife and I were dining in a restaurant in a small Chinese city. The Chinese patrons in the restaurant were, it seems, fascinated by my bright red hair. And so, as we ate, various groups of young Chinese people in the restaurant assembled behind me, after gaining my permission, to have a photograph taken of them with "the redhead." Tourists, then, aren't the only people gazing in foreign countries or taking photographs. The young Chinese men and women who wanted photographs of themselves with my wife and me probably considered me—dare I say it—exotic. This suggests that the term *exotic* may be another way of saying *other* or *different from*.

TOURISTS AS PHOTOGRAPHERS

Stanley Milgram, a social psychologist, analyzed the importance of photography for tourists. Photography, we can say, is a way of taking the tourist gaze and making it permanent, part of the tourist's recorded experience. As such, photography can be used to recall memories of the trip. Milgram writes in his essay "The Image Freezing Machine" (1976, 7–12) that the act of taking a picture is very much like the act of seeing itself, and is something that occurs in a broad range of human situations that always involves some sort of exchange. There is, he suggests, a trade-off between the passive enjoyment of a particular moment and the process of photographing it. When a person with a camera sees a beautiful scene and stops looking at the scene to take a picture, this act may interfere with the experience being fully savored.

He suggests that the very meaning of human activities, such as travel, becomes transformed by photographic possibilities. People seek out places not only for their beauty but also because they provide suitable backgrounds for their pictures. Thus a group of tourists, Nikons hanging about their necks, sees its arrival at the Eiffel tower as the consummation of a photographic quest. The place actually becomes secondary to its photographic potential.

The value of our vacation will depend, then, he concludes, not only on what we experience at a particular moment but also on how it all comes out in the pictures. It has been suggested that this contamination of the pleasurable present by the photographic urge is prompting growing numbers of vacationers to leave their cameras at home.

Milgram's point, that many people seem to go touring as if the only thing they want to do is find suitable photo opportunities, is well made and probably does apply to some tourists. But on the tours I've taken, the tourists were intent on having the best of both worlds—seeing beautiful and interesting places and taking photographs of these places, even if it meant taking a short break from sightseeing to take photographs. The development of video cameras, digital cameras, and point and shoot cameras has made the interruptions caused by capturing images much less significant now than it was in earlier years.

Some tourism scholars have suggested that taking photographs of foreign lands and people is a form of colonialism. Thus, in *Culture and the Ad: Exploring Otherness in the World of Advertising*, William M. O'Barr discusses a book by Lisl Dennis, *How to Take Better Travel Photos*, which he describes as an example of "photographic colonialism":

> No matter how innocent Dennis may think her motives are, what she describes here is *photographic colonialism*. The similarities to economic and political colonialism are remarkable. We are instructed in this manual that people who live in other parts of the world are the raw materials for our photographs. Since they are neither using their own images nor seem to care or object, we may appropriate them. (1994, 41)

Her book calls to mind, O'Barr says, the idea that "all the world's a movie set" and that "the quaintness of people's lives exists, at least in part, as subject matter for the tourist's photographs."

There is, we must recognize, often an asymmetrical power relationship between tourists and native peoples in foreign countries, a subtle sense of dominance on the part of those who can capture images, especially of "quaint" people from third world postcolonial countries. Tourists and native peoples often meet one another now in what Mary Louise Pratt, in *Imperial Eyes: Travel Writing and Transculturation*, has called "combat zones," places where people from different cultures "meet, clash and grapple with each other." For some tourists, the world isn't so much a movie set but a collection of tourism destinations that yield, for tourists (generally stereotyped in cartoons with cameras around their necks), good photo opportunities. I don't think this is the case for most tourists, however.

THE SEARCH FOR AUTHENTICITY

One of the major debates in the field of tourism studies involves the matter of the tourist's search for authenticity. Dean MacCannell deals with this subject in *The Tourist*:

> I have found the solidarity of modernity to be grounded in objective relations, in history and social facts. But unique to the modern world is its capacity to transform material relations into symbolic expressions and back again, while continuing to differentiate or multiply structures. The expansion of alternative realities makes the *dialectics of authenticity* the key to the development of the modern world. The question of authenticity transcends and subsumes the old divisions of man vs. Society, normal vs. Deviant, worker vs. Owner. (1976, 145)

So authenticity emerges, for MacCannell, as a seemingly all-powerful desire in people, particularly in tourists, to see life "as it is really lived." (Other scholars, you will see, disagree with MacCannell about the importance of authenticity.)

Is the search for authenticity the basic reason for tourism? Daniel Boorstin, in his book *The Image*, argues that modern tourists tend to be shallow individuals who are essentially in search of entertainment and are satisfied by the fake "pseudo-event" experiences sold to them by the tourist industry. Boorstin makes a distinction between tourists and travelers:

> the traveller . . . was working at something: the tourist is a pleasure-seeker. The traveller was active: he went strenuously in search of people, of adventure, of experience. The tourist is passive: he expects interesting things to happen to him. He goes sightseeing. (1961, 114)

Boorstin offers a number of distinctions between travelers and tourists, but there is some question about how valid they are. For Boorstin, it would seem that tourists are couch potatoes who move. They are searching primarily for entertainment and are easily satisfied by pseudo-authenticity or ersatz-authenticity.

In *The Tourist*, MacCannell suggests that Boorstin expresses a typical feeling tourists have—of dislike for *other* tourists. Tourists are caught up in a fundamentally ironic situation—they want to go to interesting and exotic places but where there aren't other tourists. Or perhaps, as my discussion of consumer cultures will suggest, tourists who are not like them. This places a premium on discovering new "in" or "hot" places to go before mass tourism arrives.

MacCannell suggests that modern tourists seek authenticity in other lands as a means, among other things, of gaining insights into their own lives. He agrees, however, with Boorstin's notion that the tourist industry often provides staged or inauthentic experiences and fake history that naive tourists, searching for authenticity, accept as real.

Both Boorstin and MacCannell seem to believe that tourists are passive, gullible, and easily fooled by the fake pseudo-experiences the travel industry provides them. There is no proof that this is always—or even often—the case, and while there are many tourist traps and while some tourists are gullible, to generalize the way Boorstin and MacCannell do is difficult to defend. Many tourists, I would suggest, can recognize the difference between real and staged experiences; and others—if the postmodern theorists are right—don't care very much about whether their experiences are "real" or "fake." They want to have fun and see both kinds of experiences as part of what they are looking for, which might be described as play and amusement.

The fact of the matter is that tourists are attracted to places that they find beautiful, that have cultural sites of interest, and that help them escape from the patterns they follow in their regular lives. Generally speaking, if a place is full of tourists it is because there are attractions worth seeking out. I can recall a short bus trip my wife and I took during a recent trip to Puerto Vallarta. It was to a town that shall be nameless—a forty-five-minute bus ride from Puerto Vallarta. We were the only tourists on the bus, and for good reason.

There was nothing of interest in that town at all. It was a nondescript town with nothing that would attract anyone, unless you wished to see an authentic small and uninteresting Mexican town at the end of a road to nowhere. So authenticity isn't enough—you must have something authentic that is worth seeing. Thus, tourists face two extremes: the inauthentic "staged" native culture that Boorstin writes about and the authentic but uninteresting "real" culture that I discovered at the end of our long bus ride to the Mexican town. But tourists can find pleasure and satisfaction in a lot of places in between these two extremes. It's very much like eating in a crowded restaurant. There usually are good reasons why some restaurants are crowded and others are empty.

POSTMODERNISM AND TOURISM

Postmodernism is difficult to explain, but one of its main notions is that the old, overarching philosophical principles that guided us in the past are no longer acceptable. Connected with this is the belief that the distinctions we used to make between elite culture and popular culture and between the original and the copy, between real and fake, are no longer valid. Everything becomes mixed up: the pastiche is the dominant metaphor of the age and eclecticism rules.

One of the most important philosophers of postmodernism, Jean-François Lyotard writes the following in his book *The Postmodern Condition: A Report on Knowledge*: "Simplifying to the extreme, I define *postmodern* as incredulity towards metanarratives" (1984, xxiv). He also writes about the eclectic nature of life in contemporary postmodern societies:

> Eclecticism is the degree zero of contemporary general culture: one listens to reggae, watches a western, eats McDonald's food for lunch and local cuisine for dinner, wears Paris perfume in Tokyo and "retro" clothes in Hong Kong; knowledge is a matter for TV games. It is easy to find a public for eclectic works. By becoming kitsch, art panders to the confusion which reigns in the "taste" of patrons. Artists, gallery owners, critics and the public wallow together in the "anything goes," and the epoch is one of slackening. (1984, 76)

What Lyotard describes is a culture in which the tourist ethos, of having been to many places and taken from them what one desires, leads to an eclectic lifestyle—a mix of the foreign (McDonald's) and the native (local cuisine). Behind this, of course, is the almighty dollar or euro or whatever currency one might wish to name. As Lyotard points out, this realism of the "anything goes" is in fact that of money; in the absence of aesthetic criteria, it remains possible and useful to assess the works of art according to the profit they yield. Such realism accommodates all tendencies, just as capital accommodates all "needs," providing that the tendencies and needs have purchasing power. As for taste, there is no need to be delicate when one speculates or entertains oneself. (1997, 76)

So, in the final analysis, money provides the unifying aspect behind the eclecticism of contemporary postmodern societies.

For postmodernist tourists, then, authenticity is not of any great concern, and many tourists have other interests and concerns. (It is difficult, I should point out, to define authenticity in a way that everyone will agree with.) It is reasonable to suggest that definitions of tourists as authenticity-seeking, passive, simple-minded, kitsch-loving, gullible, easily fooled, and easily satisfied are based on ideological considerations and the mind-set and political beliefs of critics and writers who make these arguments.

To title a book *The Tourist*, the way MacCannell did, is to suggest that there exists an ideal type of tourist, that all tourists are more or less the same. It is more realistic, I believe, to suggest that tourists have many different interests and reasons for travel and that no single motivation covers all of them. Their motives are as eclectic as their lifestyles.

THE POSTMODERNIST THEORY OF SIMULATIONS AND HYPERREALITY

One of the fundamental notions connected with postmodern thought is the idea that simulations have become increasingly important and the world is increasingly characterized by what has been called the hyperreal. Steven Best and Douglas Kellner explain what simulations are and how they relate to the hyperreal in their book *Postmodern Theory: Critical Interrogations*. Discussing the theories of Jean Baudrillard, an influential postmodernist sociologist, they write:

We are now, Baudrillard claims, in a new era of simulations in which computerization, information processing, media, cybernetic control systems, and the organization of society according to simulation codes and models replace production as the organizing principle of society. If modernity is the era of production controlled by the industrial bourgeoisie, the postmodern era of simulations by contrast is an era of information and signs governed by models, codes and cybernetics. Baudrillard describes "the passage from a *metallurgic* into a

semiurgic society" (1981, 185) in which signs take on a life of their own and con-
stitute a new social order structured by models, codes, and signs. "Radical semi-
urgy" describes the dramatic proliferation of signs which come to dominate
social life. . . . In a society of simulations, the models or codes structure experience and erode distinctions between the model and the real. (1991, 118–119)

Best and Kellner cite Baudrillard's use of Marshall McLuhan's theory of im-
plosion and explain that "in the postmodern world, the boundary between
image or simulation and reality implodes, and with it the very experience and
ground of 'the real' disappears" (1991, 119).

Baudrillard uses the term *hyperreal* to suggest that models and imitations
are now more real than reality. Thus Disneyland's models of the United States
are more real than the places they imitate and the United States is becoming,
Baudrillard argues, more and more like its imitation, Disneyland. The simulation becomes the model for reality.

Obviously, postmodern theories hold profound implications for our understanding of travel and tourism. In a world in which imitations are now, as
Baudrillard and many postmodernists assert, more real than reality, the
tourist's quest for authenticity is doomed or irrelevant—except that, as postmodernists might explain, the fake authenticity of the quaint village and many
similar sites are now more real than what they imitate.

SEMIOTICS AND TOURISM

In the postmodern view of things, signs have become all-important. Ferdinand de Saussure, whom I quoted earlier about the importance of differences
in making sense of concepts, also deals with signs in his book on linguistics.
He explains that a sign is composed of a sound or image, what he calls a *signifier*, and the concept connected to the sound or image, what he calls a *signified*. What is important, he adds, is that the relationship between signifier and
signified is arbitrary, based on convention. So we need to learn what signs
mean, and they can change their meaning over time.

Another theorist of signs, American philosopher Charles Sanders Peirce,
suggests that a sign "is something which stands for something to somebody in
some respect or capacity," bringing the person involved with the sign into the
equation. He also believes that the universe is "perfused with signs, if it is not
composed exclusively of signs." Semiotics, the science of signs, is an imperial-
istic science. The word *semeion*, which is at the root of *semiotics*, means sign.

A contemporary semiotician, Umberto Eco, adds an important insight—if signs can be used to tell the truth, they also can be used to lie.

Thus the sign becomes a central concern for a semiotic understanding of tourism, and many critics of mass tourism argue that it reduces itself down in the final analysis to the consumption, in one form or another, of signs—beautiful vistas, people in foreign lands in native garb, foreign cuisines, and so on. Tourism becomes, ultimately, a succession of photo opportunities.

But if the universe is composed of signs, what's a poor tourist to do? And if the boundary between the real and the imitation and between the authentic and the pseudo-authentic is irrelevant in a postmodern world of simulations, chastising tourists for being duped by the inauthentic rings rather hollow.

THE SEARCH FOR THE EXOTIC

One of the dominant goals for many tourists is finding what might be called the exotic. The term *exotic* comes from the Greek word *exotikos*, which means "outside." For tourists, the exotic means some combination of remote, unusual, different, foreign, charming, fascinating, enchanting, distant in time, intriguing, and sexual. (Stripteasers are considered exotic dancers, which explains the sexual connection.) To the extent that tourists are searching for something different from their everyday lives, the exotic represents the most distant polarity.

In the popular mind, I would suggest that certain primitive cultures and various South American, African, and Asian cultures are seen as exotic by Americans. The French may be different from us, but they are not exotic, whereas certain people in places such as Africa, India, and Southeast Asia, where dress and cuisine and architecture differ greatly from American society, are seen as exotic.

In table 2.1, I offer some attributes of the exotic and contrast it with its polar opposite, everyday life for the typical American tourist.

Table 2.1. Everyday Life and the Exotic Compared

Everyday Life	The Exotic
Near	Distant
The present	The past
Familiar	Strange
Modern	Ancient, traditional
The skyscraper	The hut
The supermarket	The souk
Cathedrals	Hindu temples, mosques
Euro-American cuisine	Ethnic cuisines
Electronic	Mechanical
Suits, dresses	Turbans, robes, costumes

Of course, the exotic comes in different forms, but generally it involves some combination of that which is strange to us, distant in place and time from us, and traditional rather than modern, as these phenomena apply to such things as landscape, architecture, dress, food, languages, and cuisines.

In Vietnam, the little tribal girls who clustered around us in Sapa, in their traditional Black Hmong and Red Zhao costumes, were exotic. They were illiterate, but many spoke four or five languages. And they dressed in costumes of their peoples that hadn't changed in hundreds of years. The northern Vietnamese resort city of Sapa, full of restaurants and hotels, was not exotic, being a typical tourist resort area (originally settled by the French) and not terribly different from what you might find anywhere.

So sometimes you find a mixture of the exotic and the ordinary in the same place. In Morocco, for example, a city such as Casablanca is very European, and therefore similar to our everyday experiences, while some places in Morocco are quite exotic, such as the souk in Fez or the Place Djemaa el Fna in Marrakech.

PILGRIMAGES

A pilgrimage is commonly understood to be travel for religious purposes: one goes to a holy site—a town, a city, a building, or a place—where it is possible to reaffirm and strengthen one's identity with one's religion or with some important figure or figures from that religion. Along the way, a person on a pilgrimage might visit other holy sites or visit places of cultural interest, but the goal of a person on a pilgrimage primarily is to visit a place that has religious significance.

As an example, let me quote from Samuel Jemsel (Adler 1930, 329), who explains why he undertook his travels:

> I was possessed by a violent and insatiable desire to visit the places of God . . . as I had learnt that eminent men such as Rabbi Isaac and Rabbi Solomon Levi had also been inflamed with the desire of accomplishing the holy journey. I, being urged on like them by a sort of divine instinct, did not lose sight of the execution of my project: I would not have suffered myself to be turned aside from it by any reason whatsoever. The desire to set out which had formed itself in my mind was so violent that it was impossible for me to remain in my own home, or to go about my accustomed business.

Jemsel's religious passion overwhelmed everything else in his life and so he undertook a pilgrimage to visit "the places of God."

In Durkheim's book *The Elementary Forms of Religious Life*, he shows how religious thought divides the world into two opposing spheres—the sacred and the profane:

> All known religious beliefs, whether simple or complex, present one common characteristic: they presupposed a classification of all things, read and ideal, of which men think, into two classes or opposed groups, generally designated by two distinct terms which are translated well enough by the words *profane* and *sacred* (profane, sacred). (1965, 52)

It is possible, then, to distinguish between pilgrimages and ordinary travel, as table 2.2 shows.

It is religious belief that motivates the pilgrim, in contrast to the desire for pleasure, entertainment, and edification that is behind conventional travel.

One makes a pilgrimage to holy sites because it is one's duty to do so, though one might also wish to do so. It is, in essence, a superego-inspired phenomenon. Touristic travel, on the other hand, is essentially an id kind of experience; one travels to satisfy one's curiosity, to have wonderful experiences, to visit important cultural sites or spectacular natural-wonder sites. The goal is pleasure and self-realization, in contrast to that of people on pilgrimages, which involve identification with the divine in historically important religious places and with important dead or living religious figures.

If Baudrillard is correct, and we now feel it is a duty to have pleasure and fun, then there is a kind of ironic reversal of Puritanism and ascetic Protestantism

Table 2.2.   Pilgrimages Contrasted with Regular Travel

Pilgrimage	Regular Travel
Sacred space	Profane space
Religious	Secular
Faith	Pleasure, edification
Superego	Id
Reinforcement	Self-realization
Identification	Curiosity
Shrines	Sites

found in travel. Touristic travel now takes on a hidden or subliminal religious quality and has elements of the sacred pilgrimage in it.

If the pilgrim seeks a holy place, this demonstrates that space can be divided between sacred space and profane space. Sacred space is, existentially, in the "center of the world" for the religious person on a pilgrimage, and profane space is always on the periphery. Some of the most well-known sacred cities are Mecca, Jerusalem, and Vatican City, but even within these holy cities some sites are more important than others. Thus, within Jerusalem, for example, the Church of the Holy Sepulchre is generally considered to be of paramount importance for Christians and the same applies to the Temple Wall, also known as the Wailing Wall, for Jews and the Dome of the Rock for Muslims.

It is possible, and it is often the case, that tourists visit sacred religious sites in the course of their travels, but these sites do not have the same meaning for tourists that they do for those on pilgrimages. For tourists, religious sites may be beautiful, interesting, and historically important, but these sites don't have the sacred significance or power to create religious fervor, or in some cases ecstasy, that they do for people on pilgrimages.

TRAVEL AS A RITE OF PASSAGE FOR YOUNG MEN AND WOMEN

Several hundred years ago, young men from wealthy families in Europe often took what was known as "the grand tour" of Europe, and in some cases, other destinations. It was held that at a certain age, travel would give young men a certain amount of polish and sophistication, as a result of their spending time in some of the great cities and visiting important museums and other cultural venues. The grand tour was, obviously, part of an elitist "rite of passage." Women were not traditionally sent on the grand tour because, in those days, women were supposed to be "sheltered" and the tour was not felt to be of importance to them in their future roles as mothers and homemakers.

This grand tour no longer is reserved for the elite, and now legions of young men and women from countries all over the world travel extensively. For example, American high school students frequently travel to Europe during summers, and many college students now take their junior year abroad. It is a modernized version of the grand tour that has been democratized and massified, but the purposes are the same—to broaden and educate young men and women by exposing them to other cultures. They visit great museums, they experience other cultures, they eat different foods, and they have adventures.

In addition, it is felt that traveling abroad and, even better, living abroad help young men and women gain an appreciation of their native culture. In fact, among middle-class students in America, going abroad is not seen as something remarkable but is taken for granted. *Not* traveling abroad is considered surprising now, and those who do not travel tend to be seen as, somehow, deprived.

Travel abroad now seems to be part of the transition from youth to adulthood; during travel, one is in what anthropologist Victor Turner calls a "liminal" state. He defines liminality in his book *Dramas, Fields and Metaphors: Symbolic Action in Human Society* (1974, 232) as "ambiguous, neither here nor there, betwixt and between all fixed points of classifications."

The foreign travels of high school and college students are, then, ritual activities tied to their liminality that mark the period in which their childhood is ending and young adulthood is dawning. After their travel, these students will be reintegrated into their communities and societies but will have a different status. Rites of passages are generally sacred in nature, connected with important changes in people's lives. They help, in this case (or so it is assumed), with the transition into adulthood.

TRAVEL AGENTS

Before the widespread use of the Internet, travel agents played a much more important role in helping people arrange travel and decide what countries and cities to visit, if one wished to take a trip abroad. Travel agents still are used by many people for that purpose—as experts who can give good advice and who can smooth out all the wrinkles and take care of all the details involved in foreign travel.

Now, with the Internet, people can get information on foreign travel agencies, hotels, restaurants, and anything else they want to know for just about any place you can imagine. In a process of disintermediation, travel agents are being pushed to the sidelines. It is possible to visit Internet sites by travel book publishers such as Rough Guides or Lonely Planet and obtain a considerable amount of information on matters such as the weather, currency, costs, hotels, museums, medical issues, and attractions of a foreign country. If you go to a search engine such as Google and type in "Vietnam Travel" or "Bali Travel" or

"Paris Travel" you get a multitude of sites that provide an enormous amount of information, so the importance of travel agents is slowly being negated for many travelers.

People generally consider "word of mouth" to be the best and most reliable information. Some travel agents, who have been to cities and countries people are thinking of visiting, can provide reassurance and generally can connect travelers with the kinds of tours that are most suitable for them. So travel agents still play a role in the scheme of things for some people—especially those who do not access the Internet.

Travel agents play other roles as well. When my wife and I decided to take a cruise to Alaska, we booked our cruise with a travel agent that specialized in cruises and that provided many different services to us. First, the cruise line made an error in announcing prices, and our travel agent picked up on this mistake and got us each a $100 reduction in the amount we paid for the cruise. In addition, because our travel agent booked a large number of people on the ship (approximately 150 people), everyone who booked with our agent was treated to special cocktail parties, kitchen tours, and bridge tours. We also got flowers, free sweatshirts, and boxes of candy. So sometimes there is good reason to use travel agents, and in the case of cruises, most people who book cruises use travel agents specializing in that kind of travel, some of whom they find on the Internet. The cruise lines actually encourage people to use travel agents.

I booked an "adventure tour" of Vietnam with a Vietnamese travel agency that I located through the Internet. I checked with several travel guidebooks, which mentioned the agency as being first-rate, so I felt it wasn't a big risk to book with them. It turned out to be an extremely good choice and a great deal less expensive than if I had booked my tour with an American agency. So travel agencies and companies that arrange tours for people continue to play an important role in the travel industry.

AN IMAGE THAT EXPLAINS THINGS

The best way to visualize the complexity of the travel industry is to imagine, in your mind's eye, a person—a tourist—standing in the middle of a large room. Circling around that tourist are people who do certain things or represent certain industries related to travel. I am talking about cab drivers, bus drivers, train conductors, airline pilots, cruise ship captains, clothing manufacturers, travel agents, tour company representatives, hotel clerks, local guides, guidebook publishers, owners of restaurants, museum docents, symphony orchestra musicians, dancers and singers from night clubs, players from baseball teams and other sports teams, clerks from gambling casinos . . . the list goes on and on.

So when John Doe calls up his travel agent and says he and his wife want to book a two-week tour of Spain, that decision is connected to many different people and institutions all over the world. In a certain sense, travel is simple— but that's because so many institutions, in various places all over the world, are available to take care of the needs and desires of travelers and tourists.

In a vast portion of human history, men have been the travelers; and travel literature is—with a few significant, and often modern exceptions—a male literature reflecting a masculine point of view. This comes as no surprise to those who have digested the insistence of modern feminists that men have generated and monopolized representational realities in which the voice of women is silent, undercut, or assumed. In the history of patriarchal civilizations—and, as yet, there are no other kinds—humanity has worn the mask of masculinity and travel has been a performance of this persona.

The masculinization of motion and the feminization of sessility [being attached] are clearly products of cultural patterning, many examples of which occur through the travel literature. In patriarchal cultures, the mobility of men—especially of young, unattached men—is overdetermined and powerfully charged by the reigning images of masculinity, whether of the wandering knight or of the wandering holy man, the shaman or the actor.

—*Eric J. Leed*, The Mind of the Traveler: From Gilgamesh to Global Tourism

The Uses of Travel and Tourism

In this chapter, I deal with the uses people make of travel and tourism and with various demographic considerations related to travel. I have already dealt with a number of matters connected with tourism, from travel in the Bible to travel agents. I will begin this chapter with a consideration of the gratifications provided by travel and tourism.

GRATIFICATIONS OF TRAVEL

In my previous chapter, I dealt with Jean Baudrillard's suggestion that we now feel compelled to have fun and thus there is, in terms of our interests in this book, a subliminal compulsion to travel. But if there is a "push" to tourism because of this need to have fun, there is also a "pull" in terms of desire for the gratifications travel provides.

Communication scholars developed the theory of uses and gratifications to explain how audiences use media. This theory was a reaction against theories that focused on how media affect audiences. We can adapt this theory of uses and gratifications to consider how people might be using travel and what gratifications travel provides. Let me suggest some of the gratifications of travel.

To Be Amused and Entertained

We wish to see what the world has to offer in the way of experiences that we will find entertaining and pleasurable. This might involve dining in a restaurant in a foreign land, going to a spectacle such as a bullfight in Spain, or watching a performance of folk dancing. One of the most important ways tourists entertain themselves is shopping for objects that will remind them of their experiences in foreign lands and which, they assume (not always correctly), will be a bargain.

To Experience the Beautiful

One of the main delights of travel is to visit beautiful cities, such as Paris or Vienna, and parts of countries—such as the desert in Morocco, spectacular islands, pristine beaches, and the like that are beautiful and that we find spiritually uplifting.

To Have a Sense of the Fellowship of Men and Women

Many people, especially the people Mary Douglas describes as egalitarians, derive a great deal of pleasure from interacting with people in other countries and gaining a sense of fellowship and community with them.

To Satisfy Curiosity and Gain Information about the World

Human beings are naturally curious, and travelers are human beings who act on their curiosity and desire for information and experience about what life in other lands is like. Even travelers who visit countries for a short period of time can get insights about foreign countries if they are perceptive.

To Participate in History

People have a desire to participate in history, which explains why they wish to be at important sporting events or visit places where great historical events took place or great historical figures lived and worked. People want to connect themselves to places and events of importance; tourism—visiting Freud's home or visiting the Great Mosque in Istanbul or the Bastille—is one way people can do this. This is an attempt to deal with the anxiety most people have about the fact that their lives, as J. William Fulbright once explained, are minor events in the ongoing universe.

To Obtain Outlets for Sexual Drives in a Guilt-Free Manner

Unfortunately, sexual tourism and exploitation is an important element in the travel industry, even though governments in countries where it exists try (or claim they try) to curtail it. Many travelers feel that having sex with women in foreign countries is not morally problematic; thus, for example, there used to be sex tours for Japanese men in Thailand. In like manner, many males from foreign lands feel that having sex with women travelers is perfectly acceptable and even desirable as a means, among other things, of getting back at those who they feel are exploiting them.

To Gain an Identity

Traveling gives people an identity. People who do a great deal of traveling become, whatever else they may be, "world travelers." They often use this identity, which has positive connotations, when interacting with others. They find ways to introduce the subject when they meet new people. Travel allows those who have traveled to demonstrate a certain amount of expertise ("I know of a wonderful restaurant on the Left Bank"), suggests an adventurous character ("Part of the road was washed out, so everyone on the bus got out and found rocks to rebuild the road"), and also provides a subject for people to talk about that is innocuous and unlikely to lead to arguments.

We see, then, that people who travel derive a number of benefits from the experience, which helps explain why tourism is such an enormous industry. As the quotation that begins this chapter points out, travel has, for most of recorded history, been something that men did. But that is changing.

TRAVEL AND GENDER

A number of factors play a part in women starting to travel. One thing is the development of mass tourism and the various technologies connected with mass tourism, such as the airplane, the ocean liner, the railroad, the automobile, and the bus. These new transportation technologies have made it possible for women to travel in numbers similar to that of men.

There is also the matter of a change in our attitudes toward women and changes in the way children are raised. Women are no longer "sessile," to use Leed's term—and women travelers are no longer unusual. You need only look at travelers in any large airport to see that women make up a large part of the traveling public—and not just women from Western countries. In international airports you see women from all over the world. This change is tied to modernization and to changes in attitudes caused, in part, by modernization and the fact that more and more women are getting access to education.

In addition, we must consider the role feminist theories have had in giving women a sense of liberation from the constraints of everyday life and of empowering them. There is no reason why women can't be explorers and world travelers, and many are. As I mentioned earlier, my own "wanderlust" was stimulated by an art teacher, who often talked about her adventures in India and other far-off lands when I studied with her in the 1940s. She was, perhaps, ahead of her time, but the spirit of adventure lives in women as much as it does in men—and some would say more than it does in men, who, market research has found, tend to be somewhat conservative in purchasing vacations. These factors may help explain why we see so many women traveling nowadays—sometimes to see what they can of the world before they settle down and at other times because they have the time, the money, and the freedom to travel.

TRAVEL, SOCIOECONOMIC CLASS, AND CONSUMER CULTURES

According to Mary Douglas, consumer decisions are based primarily on affiliation with one of the four consumer cultures and antagonism toward the others. This leads to a considerable difference in tourism preferences than if tourism choices were based only on socioeconomic class. We see these differences in table 3.1.

If travel is based on decisions connected to socioeconomic class, then class differences would be paramount and the price of a trip becomes important, as a means of maintaining social distance from other classes. Presumably, class-based decisions focus on keeping distance from other classes, and decision making about what kind of travel to engage in is based on desires and other psychological phenomena.

Douglas argues that membership in one of the four consumer cultures is basic, and group affiliation—and hostility toward other consumer cultures—is the engine that drives decisions about travel and all other kinds of consumption.

Table 3.1.   Travel Preferences: Socioeconomic Class versus Consumer Culture

Socioeconomic Class	Consumer Culture
Class differences basic	Member of consumer culture basic
Money	Group strength and number of rules
Price of trip	Being with one's own consumer culture
Social distance	Avoiding other consumer cultures
Psychology: Desire	Sociological theory: Group affiliation

Psychologists tell us that people continually seek reinforcement for their beliefs, values, and attitudes and try to avoid dissonance. This would lead people to seek travel that places them with other members of their particular consumer culture, whether it be elitist, individualist, egalitarian (enclavist), or fatalist (isolate).

I am addressing here what Max Weber calls "ideal types"—and in reality, members of the four consumer cultures might mix with one another by chance or by accident or for other reasons. Let us consider, then, how the members of our four consumer cultures travel. To suggest how the four cultures differentiate themselves from one another, I will identify some popular cultural phenomena (books, popular songs), followed by where travelers go on trips, what they do, what arrangements they make if they wish to travel by ship, and where they eat when abroad (see table 3.2).

This table is a bit fanciful, but it shows the differences between how members of the different consumer cultures might—if everything went perfectly—travel. My examples of the kinds of books that members of each consumer culture read and the songs they prefer suggest that people in each of these consumer cultures consider different things to be important, and members in these groups gain identity, as Douglas puts it, by not being like people in the other consumer cultures. Let me slightly modify what she asserts about shopping by substituting the word *travel* for *shopping:* "Travel is agonistic, a struggle to define not what one is but what one is not." Deciding what kind of travel to undertake and what arrangements to make for travel is, of course, a form of shopping.

Table 3.2.   Travel and Consumer Cultures

Elitist	Individualist	Egalitarian	Fatalist
The Prince	Looking Out for Number One	I'm Okay, You're Okay	1984
God Save the Queen	I Did It My Way	We Are the World	Anarchy in the U.K.
England and European capitals	Offbeat places such as Laos	Cuba, China	Visits to relatives
Tours of great houses	Adventure	Ecotourism	Short trips by car or bus
Luxury cruises	Sailboats	Ferries to Alaska	Camping
Dine with friends in their houses in foreign cities	Restaurants	Cafeterias	Picnics

TRAVEL AND AGE

Anyone who has done much traveling abroad can recall seeing legions of young men and women, with big backpacks, wandering around railroad stations and airline terminals. Young people, often with limited budgets but plenty of time, tend to travel in as economical a manner as possible and stay in youth hostels and inexpensive hotels. Middle-aged and elderly people generally travel differently, having more money and less energy. So the way people travel is affected, among other things, by their age.

Cruise lines face a problem in that many people perceive cruises as only for elderly rich people. In actuality, there is often a rough breakdown in which one-third of the passengers on a cruise are young, one-third are middle aged, and one-third are elderly; many people who take cruises are middle and lower middle class in terms of their incomes. If you look at many of the brochures that cruise lines send to prospective passengers, you see that many thirtyish people grace the photographs, along with the traditional gray-haired and sixtyish executive-looking types and their glamorous middle-aged wives.

Many people do a great deal of traveling after they retire, when they have unlimited time and adequate resources and can take advantage of bargains during off-season periods. So age is an important factor in tourism, one that those who work in the tourism industry take into consideration. People who like to travel tend to travel when they are young, cut down on their traveling when they have children, resume their traveling when their children are older, and travel a good deal when they have retired and have the time and financial resources to do so.

TRAVEL AND ETHNICITY

A considerable amount of tourism involves people from ethnic groups visiting their ethnic homelands as a means of reaffirming their ethnic identities. On the other hand, many tourists are interested in visiting places where ethnic identity is strong, to have authentic experiences and to satisfy their curiosity about other ways of living. So ethnicity plays an important role in travel.

In the United States, the melting pot metaphor was used for many years to describe the way people from foreign ethnic groups were allegedly assimilated (or, perhaps, *dissolved* might be a better term) into American culture. This metaphor has been replaced by another one, the "beef stew" metaphor, which recognizes that the numerous ethnic groups in the United States have not "melted" away but have maintained their ethnic identities at the same time that they have adopted many American values and beliefs. The new image of America is of a multicultural country, with many different ethnic, racial, and religious groups living together, relatively harmoniously.

The multiethnicity of the United States (and the same applies to many other countries as well, nowadays) has led to a proliferation of ethnically focused travel agencies that cater to ethnic groups that wish to travel—either back to their countries of origin or elsewhere—and who wish to do so with the help of an agent of their same ethnicity. An agent of their own ethnicity, they feel, probably understands their needs and desires better than someone who does not share their ethnic identity and can communicate with them more easily.

In *The Tourist*, Dean MacCannell suggests that "modernized people, released from primary family and ethnic group responsibilities, organize themselves in groups around worldviews provided by cultural productions" (1976, 30). I would question this assertion and suggest that people in contemporary multicultural countries, such as the United States, France, and Great Britain, may be modernized, but they still maintain their ethnic identities and their ethnicity plays a significant role in their travel and tourism.

TRAVELERS AS RISK TAKERS

Travel always involves elements of risk since things often go wrong when you travel—your flight is delayed and you miss your connecting flight, or the bus you are traveling on breaks down. These things that go wrong are generally inconveniences, not serious risks, but the fact remains that it takes a certain personality to travel. You must expect that, for one reason or another, something might go wrong and be willing to deal with the problems that arise. Many people are risk-averse and either don't travel or find ways of traveling, such as taking group tours, that minimize risk as much as possible.

German sociologist Georg Simmel was interested in what he called "adventures." He explains that an adventure involves dropping out, for a precise period, of the continuity of life, of the regularities and certainties that are part of our everyday lives. Simmel adds that adventures take on the qualities of dreams in our psychic life, and they have much sharper beginnings and endings than other aspects of our experience, which helps explain why we remember them so vividly. It is this capacity to accept the role of risk and chance in our lives that connects the traveler and the adventurer. And because our travels and adventures are so exhilarating, we remember them quite vividly.

Since the tragic events of September 11, 2001, assessments of risk play an ever-increasing role in travel. When we become tourists we make what might be described as a hedonistic calculus (or risk–benefit analysis) in which we try to balance the expenditures we will be making in time and money and the risks involved in taking a trip with the pleasures we expect to experience.

Tourists need to consider any number of factors relative to risk in planning their trips—everything from terrorism to possible illnesses and, in particular, the outbreak of dangerous diseases, such as SARS (Severe Acute Respiratory Syndrome). Terrorism, for example, has devastated tourism in Israel and Bali, and the SARS outbreak in 2003 had a major impact on tourism in Toronto, Canada, and in many countries in Asia. The fact that tourism rebounded so quickly after the SARS epidemic was contained indicates how important tourism, along with the need for travel and a momentary escape from familiar reference points, is in everyone's lives.

TRAVELERS AS STRANGERS

Simmel also points out that strangers—people who are new to some place—tend to see things that don't attract the attention of natives or are almost invisible to natives. Strangers can be more objective than natives. That's because the reference points for strangers are new and the customs and traditions that are part of the lives of natives are not familiar to strangers, and thus of some interest. The natives are so used to things that they pay no attention to behaviors, rites, and customs that, to strangers (such as anthropologists and tourists), are often quite remarkable.

So travelers are people who put themselves—if only for short periods of time—in the situation of being strangers and who derive enjoyment from this status. Being a stranger means travelers must be more active, find ways to make sense of foreign things, and figure out how to take care of basic necessities. This has certain psychological benefits in making the traveler feel more alive and resourceful, but it is only possible when the place being visited is not too far removed from what the traveler is used to; if travelers don't know the language being spoken, and know nothing about the culture at all, they need help—from guides and other people who see to it that travelers are taken care of. Being a stranger has its difficulties, but it also has its pleasures, and that pleasure—of investigating that which is strange and seeing things for oneself—is one of the strongest motivations for travel.

TRAVEL AND NOSTALGIA FOR THE PAST

One element of travel, which often involves going to sites of great historic interest, can be explained as a kind of longing for the imagined wonders of the past and of what travel was like during this time.

Thus, the great French anthropologist Claude Lévi-Strauss laments that he didn't have a chance to experience "real" travel:

> I should have liked to live in the age of *real* travel, when the spectacle on offer had not yet been blemished, contaminated, and confounded; then I could have seen Lahore not as I saw it, but as it appeared to Bernier, Tavernier, Manucci. . . . There's no end, of course, to such conjectures. When was the right moment to see India? At what period would the study of the Brazilian savage have yielded the purest satisfaction and the savage himself have been at his peak? . . . The alternative is inescapable: either I am a traveller in ancient times, and faced with a prodigious spectacle which would be almost entirely unintelligible to me and might, indeed, provoke me to mockery or disgust; or I am a traveller of our own day, hastening in search of a vanished reality. (1970, 44–45)

This nostalgia for the days when there was such a thing as real travel and the sense that travel hadn't been corrupted by mass tourism haunts Lévi-Strauss's book. *Tristes Tropiques* is now considered a classic travel book, though he announces in his book that he loathes travel.

Bill Buford, who edited a collection of travel articles published in *Granta* magazine, comments about the effect of modernization on travel, lamenting that the Second World War marked the end of travel as we used to know it and the beginning of mass tourism:

> World War Two marked the end of the great age of travel. And it is easy to see why. Not only did the war make travel difficult, but the world that emerged after

it—a monoculture of mass consumerism, package-holidays and the extraordinary imperialism of the American hamburger—left little room for the sensibility characteristic of so many of the writers of the twenties and thirties. The books of Robert Byron, say, or Waugh, Auden, and Priestly are virtually Edwardian in temperament: they hark back to an earlier time. They wrote, as Paul Fussell has pointed out in *Abroad*, to celebrate a "Golden Age": the corners of the world uncontaminated by the manifestations of modernity. "One travelled," Fussell says, "to discover the past." (1984)

This "past," of course, was one enjoyed by the elite. Soon the world was to be "contaminated" by the gastronomic imperialism of Coca-Cola and the American hamburger and the development of mass tourism, forcing the world to put up with the horrors of hordes of "ugly" middle-class Americans.

TRAVEL AND AMBIVALENCE TOWARD MODERNITY

Connected to this nostalgia for the possibility of "real" travel in the past is a nostalgia for what I would call the "imaginary" past itself, when life seemed to have been more interesting and exciting. Dean MacCannell touches on this matter in *The Tourist*:

Modernity first appears to everyone as it did to Lévi-Strauss, as disorganized fragments, alienating, wasteful, violent, superficial, unplanned, unstable and inauthentic. On second examination, however, this appearance seems almost a mask, for beneath the disorderly exterior, modern society hides a firm resolve to establish itself on a worldwide base.

Modern values are transcending the old divisions between the Communist East and the Capitalist West and between the "developed" and "third" worlds. The progress of modernity ("modernization") depends on its very sense of instability and inauthenticity. For moderns, reality and authenticity are thought to be elsewhere: in other historical periods and other cultures, in purer, simpler lifestyles. In other words, the concerns of moderns for "naturalness," their nostalgia and their search for authenticity are not merely casual and somewhat decadent, though harmless, attachments to the souvenirs of destroyed cultures and dead epochs. They are also components of the conquering spirit of modernity—the grounds of its unifying consciousness. (1976, 2–3)

This unifying consciousness is located, for MacCannell, in the middle class, which scavenges the earth for new experiences to be woven into a collective, touristic version of other peoples and other places" (1976, 13).

In the past, only the wealthy or aristocrats traveled because they were the only ones who could afford to travel. Mass tourism is now essentially a middle-class phenomenon and, for that reason, is attacked by elitists and others who, it would seem, identify either with aristocratic philosophical beliefs or Marxist and left-wing ideological beliefs. These two groups are united in despising the middle classes, and their nostalgia is tied either to a dream of the past, of an aristocratic society, when there were no middle-class people, or of the future and a utopian classless all middle-class world.

TRAVEL AS PERSONAL TRANSFORMATION

One thing that travel offers people is the ability to transform themselves in varying ways. It is generally held that travel broadens people by giving them the opportunity to see how others live and to experience great works of art of all kinds, which is commonly believed to elevate one both spiritually and emotionally. So the notion that travel can change people is a common one.

But there is a good reason to believe that travel also enables people to transform themselves in more profound ways. In our everyday lives we become locked, so to speak, in a series of relationships that offer us our identity. We gain our sense of who we are by the way others react to us, and sometimes, as a result of chance events and unfortunate circumstances, we obtain an identity that is not one we like. It is significant others, at our jobs and in our social relationships, who confer identity upon us.

Travel enables us to escape, momentarily, from the identities we have been given and to try on new identities. Paul Fussell explains this in a book he edited, *The Norton Book of Travel*:

> Why is travel so exciting? Partly because it triggers the thrill of escape, from the constriction of the daily, the job, the boss, the parents. "A great part of the pleasure of travel," says Freud, "lies in the fulfillment of . . . early wishes to escape the family and especially the father." The escape is also from the traveler's domestic identity, and among strangers a new sense of selfhood can be tried on,

like a costume. The anthropologist Claude Lévi-Strauss notes that a traveler takes a journey not just in space and time (most travel being to places more ancient than the traveler's home) but "in the social hierarchy as well"; and he has noticed repeatedly that arriving in a new place, he has suddenly become rich (travelers to Mexico, China, or India will know the feeling). The traveler's escape, at least since the Industrial Age, has also been from the ugliness and racket of Western cities, and from factories, parking lots, boring turnpikes, and roadside squalor. (1987, 13)

So travel provides escape from both personal identity and, if one goes to certain countries, class identity. When you travel to certain countries, such as China and Vietnam and a host of other countries in Asia and Southeast Asia, for a short period you become "rich" and live the way the rich do.

This escape from the social hierarchy one is caught in during everyday life helps rupture the old identity and makes it possible for travelers to assume a different identity when they return to their everyday routines. Travelers can try on their new identities "like a costume" and if they like them, adopt them, with necessary modifications when they return to their regular lives. This would suggest that travel, especially travel abroad, can have rather profound effects on people, which would explain why so many people find themselves drawn to foreign travel. They may not fully recognize the benefits they derive from this kind of travel, but they do sense that their travel has been a valuable experience.

Psychoanalytic theorists talk about the process of separation and individuation in individuals. According to this theory, people must find ways to separate themselves from the dominating influence of their parents and find a way to achieve an identity of their own. This is similar to what anthropologists talk about when they refer to separation, liminality, and achieving an identity. We see how these two theories relate to one another in table 3.3, which also deals with travel.

The two theories are similar in that there is some kind of a break with one's family and with one's childhood, a liminal period in which one is "in between"

Table 3.3. Separation in Psychoanalytic and Anthropological Theory

Psychoanalytic	Child	Separation	Individuation
Anthropological	Child	Liminality	Adulthood
Travel	Separation	Education	Transformation

childhood and adulthood, and a resolution in which a person emerges changed considerably. I am suggesting that travel may be something like these two processes. One escapes, if only for a short period, from the life one is used to. This status that the tourist experiences can be described as a liminal one. During the trip one is "educated" about the possibilities that exist for living one's life, and one's horizons are broadened. At the end of the trip, it is quite likely that travelers have undergone experiences that change, to varying degrees, their attitudes, beliefs, and values.

TRAVEL AND THE CARNIVALESQUE

Fussell suggests that one of the pleasures of travel is escape from the constrictions of daily life and the chance to try on new identities. One other element of travel related to this matter of personal identity needs explanation, and that is the relationship between travel and what Russian cultural theorist Mikhail Bakhtin describes as the "carnivalesque." In his book *Rabelais and His World,* published in Russian in 1965 and in English in 1984, Bahktin explains his theory. His book is a study of the great writer Rabelais, author of a medieval literary work, *Gargantua and Pantagruel.* Bakhtin ties Rabelais to the values, beliefs, and celebrations of people who lived in the medieval period—and in particular to the carnival periods that were so important to them:

> Carnival is not a spectacle seen by the people; they live in it, and everyone participates because its very idea embraces all the people. While carnival lasts, there is no other life outside it. During carnival time life is subject only to its laws, that is, the laws of its own freedom. It has a universal spirit; it is a special condition of the entire world, of the world's revival and renewal, in which all take part . . . carnival is the people's second life, organized on the basis of laughter. It is a festive life. Festivity is a peculiar quality of all comic rituals and spectacles of the Middle Ages. (1984, 7–8)

Feasting, it turns out, was a very important aspect of carnivals. Feasts (and we could substitute their modern equivalent, dining) are "important primary forms of human culture." That is, many feasts, especially the official ones, allowed people to escape, for a short while—during the carnival period—from the norms of their everyday lives.

During carnival time, the numerous distinctions between people and the rules and laws that existed were suspended for a period of gaiety, licentiousness, laughter, and feasting. Bakhtin's notion of "carnivalization" helps explain, I believe, why travel and tourism are so popular. Tourism is a modern attempt, somewhat modified of course from the medieval forms of carnival, to introduce into the lives of contemporary people the sense of liberation and joy that took place during carnival time. Travel, more than any other form of leisure activity, offers an opportunity to not only change one's personality (if only for a while) but also to escape from routine and the alienation that many social sciences argue pervades contemporary society.

You find this carnivalesque sensibility especially well developed on cruises, where passengers often develop a sense of community, a sense of freedom (to eat when and where they want, to read a book, to do anything they want), a sense of equality (in that everyone, no matter whether in a lowly inside cabin or a stately suite, dines in the same dining rooms), and the modern equivalent of feasting (gourmet lunches and dinners, twenty-four-hour dining, free pizzas, and so on).

When people return from their travels, they often talk about having "recharged" their batteries, suggesting that their momentary escape from their everyday routines and their experiences in different places have had a beneficial impact on them. If everyday life had depleted their batteries, travel had recharged their batteries.

VAGABONDS AND WANDERERS

These beneficial effects of travel do not apply to all people who visit different countries. Some people—individuals and in some cases families—seem incapable of leading a "normal" life, which generally involves having a steady job, friends, and a family. These vagabonds and wanderers drift around, taking odd jobs here and there or living on remittances to sustain themselves. These individuals are victims of a compulsion (and sometimes a need) to keep moving, and it isn't really correct to describe them as travelers, for they don't have the interests of travelers. They seem interested only in moving around rather than in new cultures and new experiences.

Some psychoanalytic theorists have suggested that many drifters and wanderers are searching for an idealized mother or father figure, who, of course, they never find. Thus, they are condemned to keep moving and searching. To take Freud's notion of travel as an escape from the father, they may also be fleeing from their real or imaginary powerful fathers and searching for an idealized and imaginary "loving" father.

There are, of course, some itinerant workers who keep moving. An estimated eight or ten thousand Irish Travelers, tin workers who do odd jobs, roam the United States, and other groups of itinerant workers, such as Gypsies, exist in other lands. But they are not vagabonds and wanderers, as I have defined them.

We see, then, that travel can be a source of liberation and freedom, enabling us to temporarily (and perhaps, at times, permanently) change our identities and gain a sense of communion with others, or it can be a compulsion, forcing some poor souls to continually wander around, more or less aimlessly. For most people, the gratifications and psychological benefits that touristic travel provides make it a valuable experience in more ways than they can imagine.

Travel is a common, frequent, everyday occurrence in the present. In fact, it is a source of our commonality—in 1987 more than forty million Americans traveled abroad, and many more at home. Comprising less than 5 percent of the world's population, U.S. citizens accounted for over 25 percent of the world's spending for domestic and international travel—estimated at $2.3 trillion. If one counts all the California trips and journeys seasonally made, north and south, it is not merely a metaphor to say America is on the move and connected through mobilities. Travel, in the form of tourism, is becoming increasingly pervasive in our world. By the turn of the millennium, it will be the most important sector of world trade, surpassing oil, and is currently the second largest retail industry in the United States. The impression of the commonality of travel is intensified when one includes in the ranks of travelers those who obviously belong but do not appear in tourism statistics—business travelers, nomads, commuters, itinerant laborers, refugees, members of the armed services, diplomatic personnel, temporary and permanent immigrants.

—*Eric J. Leed*, The Mind of the Traveler: From Gilgamesh to Global Tourism

1

The Tourism Industry

As I've mentioned earlier, travelers rely on a huge infrastructure to make their trips possible, everything from cab rides to airports, airlines and cruise ships, railroads, hotels, and restaurants, to name just a few of the industries allied with the travel industry. In this chapter, I deal with some statistics about the travel industry and with related topics such as which nationalities travel the most, changes in travel, and the impact of the growth of terrorism on tourism.

SIZE OF THE TRAVEL INDUSTRY

We have to recognize that in 1998 global travel and tourism was a $3.6 trillion industry employing more than 230 million people. The World Travel and Tourism Council (the source of these figures) estimates that by 2010 travel and tourism will be an $8 trillion industry employing around 330 million people.

The World Tourism Organization offers other interesting data. International tourist arrivals went from 69 million in 1960 to 625 million in 1998, an enormous increase. Obviously, travel and tourism are of great economic importance from a global perspective. In 1998 this industry accounted for 8.2 percent of the world's gross domestic product, and it is estimated to grow to 12.5 percent by 2010.

MOST POPULAR DESTINATIONS

Let me offer statistics on world travel for 2001 from the World Tourism Organization to show some interesting aspects of international tourism. Table 4.1 lists the top ten tourist countries in terms of number of visitors (in millions) and the population of the country visited (in millions).

Table 4.1. Most Popular Tourist Destinations

Country	Visitors (in millions)	Size of Country (in millions)
France	76.5	58
Spain	49.5	40
United States	45.5	270
Italy	39.0	57
United Kingdom	23.4	58
Mexico	19.8	100
Canada	19.7	30
Austria	18.2	8
Germany	17.9	81

France gets the largest number of tourists (more than 76 million a year), but Austria is the country that attracts the largest number of tourists relative to its population—with more than 18 million tourists visiting a country of 8 million people. To put these figures in perspective, Mexico and Austria receive similar (within a million or so) visitors, but Mexico's population of 100 million people is more than twelve times larger than Austria's.

NATIONS THAT TRAVEL THE MOST

The countries that spent the most money on international travel and tourism in 1991, based on data from the World Tourism Organization, are shown in table 4.2.

These figures show why so many travelers comment that wherever they go, they find many German travelers. Germans are second, after the United States, in the amount of money they spend on tourism, and on a per capita basis, spend much more money than Americans do. Plus they have six weeks of vacation, as a rule, which gives them time to travel. Table 4.3. identifies per capita expenses on travel. This table reveals something quite interesting—

Table 4.2. Expenses on Tourism by Nations

Country	Amount spent (in billions of dollars)	Population (in millions)
United States	58.9	270
Germany	45.9	81
United Kingdom	36.9	58
Japan	31.9 (1990 figures)	120
France	17.5	58

Table 4.3. Per Capita Expenses on Tourism

Country	United States	Germany	United Kingdom	France	Japan
Expenditure	60 billion	46 billion	37 billion	17 billion	31 billion
Population	270 million	81 million	58 million	58 million	120 million
Per capita	$222	$575	$637	$293	$258
Ranking	5	2	1	3	4

while Americans spend the most for travel, on a per capita basis for travel by nations, we end up fifth and people from the United Kingdom place first, followed closely by Germans.

Proportionately, the 81 million Germans who spend $46 billion spend a great deal more, on a per capita basis, than the 270 million Americans who spend $60 billion. If, for example, there were 240 million Germans and they spent money for travel at the same rate they do now, they would spend $138 billion; so Germans spend, on average, more than twice as much for travel as Americans do. If there were 240 million people in the U.K., they would spend $150 billion, so people from the U.K. spend even more money, proportionately speaking, than Germans and are rated the number one country in terms of money spent by travelers. The Japanese come in fourth and the Americans are fifth in terms of per capita dollars spent on international travel.

KINDS OF TOURISTS: SEGMENTATION IN THE TRAVEL INDUSTRY

Tourism is an all-inclusive term that covers a multitude of different modes of travel and kinds of arrangements for touring available to people. Table 4.4 suggests some of the different possibilities for a person living in San Francisco. We could, of course, do the same for people living anywhere.

There is talk, also, of interplanetary tourism in the future—taking a rocket to the moon, though why one would want to visit the moon is beyond me. (One very wealthy tourist has actually been to the moon.) An almost infinite number of international tourism possibilities are available in

Table 4.4. Kinds of Tourism

Local Tourism	Look around San Francisco
Regional Tourism	Visit the wine country
National Tourism	Visit national parks
International Tourism	Take a cruise in Asia or a tour of Italy

addition to the more traditional ways of traveling: studying languages, taking Elderhostel courses, working on archeological digs, taking summer courses in foreign universities, hiking, biking, scuba diving, skiing, taking cooking courses in foreign countries . . . the list is endless.

There is a difference between the stereotyped tourist who takes a tour where he or she stays in five-star hotels and has nothing to do with the natives, except photograph them, and the kind of tourism that most people do. Not everyone takes organized mass tours that keep them in what Erik Cohen described as an "environmental bubble." He describes these tours in his article "Toward a Sociology of International Tourism":

> The organized mass tourist is the least adventurous and remains largely confined to his "environmental bubble" throughout his trip. The guided tour, conducted in an air conditioned bus, traveling at high speed through a streaming countryside, represents the prototype of the organized mass tourist. This tourist type buys a package tour as if it were just another commodity in the modern mass market. The itinerary for his trip is fixed in advance, and all his stops are well-prepared and guided: he makes almost no decisions for himself and stays almost exclusively in the microenvironment of his home country. Familiarity is at a maximum, novelty at a minimum. (Goeldner et al. 1999, 34)

This kind of tour still exists, but it is a stereotype of an extreme kind of international tourism. I have taken three packaged tours—in Morocco, in China, in Vietnam—and in none of the tours did I feel in an "environmental bubble." This may be because as the tourism industry has matured, the companies that offer these tours have learned how to run a structured tour yet make it possible for tourists to have a different kind of experience from the one Cohen describes.

Cohen lists four kinds of tourists in his article:

The organized mass tourist

The individual mass tourist

The explorer

The drifter

The individual mass tourist has a certain amount of control over his time and itinerary, but all of his arrangements are made through a tourist agency. He ventures out of the "environmental bubble" to interact with natives and experience the cultures he is visiting but only a bit more than the organized mass tourist. The explorer makes her own arrangements and wants to get off the beaten track and mingle with the natives, but she also wants to be comfortable and doesn't stray too far from the environmental bubble. The drifter is the polar opposite of the organized mass tourist and tries to live the way the natives do. He has no fixed itinerary and just drifts around, working at odd jobs and "going native" to the extent that this is possible.

It is possible, without doing too much violence to the facts, to tie these four kinds of tourists to the four consumer cultures elaborated by Aaron Wildavsky and Mary Douglas (see table 4.5).

Cohen's organized mass tourist, who stays in five-star hotels, is closest to the consumer culture of the elitist (in terms of the lifestyle he has while traveling, though he probably is a member of the middle class at home), and the explorer, who makes her own arrangements, is closest to the individualist. The individual mass tourist, a term that is essentially contradictory, is probably closest to the egalitarian, and the drifter is very similar to the fatalist or, in Douglas's terms, the isolate.

We move now to a discussion of changes that have taken place in the tourism industry in recent years.

CHANGES IN THE TRAVEL INDUSTRY

Many changes have taken place as the travel industry has matured. New generations of airplanes now make flying more affordable (though the hassles at airports, due to the rules put in place to prevent terrorism, are very burdensome), new "hot places" to go are constantly being discovered or created, and new kinds of arrangements for tourists, such as all-inclusive resort experiences, are being developed all the time.

Table 4.5. Cohen's Tourists Typology and Consumer Cultures

Elitist	Individualist	Egalitarian	Fatalist
Organized mass tourist	Explorer	Individual mass tourist	Drifter

One of the most remarkable changes in travel has been the development of the cruise industry. The cruise industry is an $8 billion industry now, with a 1,400 percent growth rate since 1970. Consider the statistics in table 4.6 about cruising obtained from the International Council of Cruise Lines.

In only thirty years, the number of people taking cruises increased from half a million to almost ten million and the International Council of Cruise Lines estimates that this figure will double in another ten years. Some eighty new cruise liners have been placed in service (or are being built and will be placed in service shortly) to accommodate all these people. Cruise ships now visit 1,800 ports around the world, so cruising is a truly global form of travel. It also employs around 250,000 people in the United States and many other countries, mostly from the third world, on the ships.

Like other kinds of travel, the cruise ship industry is highly segmented. In Bob Dickinson and Andy Vladimir's *Selling the Sea: An Inside Look at the Cruise Industry* (1997), we find the following categories and the cruise lines (some of which no longer exist) that fit in these categories (see table 4.7).

Because of the large number of cruise ships and overcapacity in the industry, there is a great deal of competition by the cruise lines to fill their cabins (which is how they make money). It is not unusual to see some cruises advertised for as little at $50 per person, per day, for inside cabins.

We can see, then, from the example of cruising, that the travel industry is a dynamic one, with an almost infinite number of tours and travel arrangements available for people with different tastes and incomes. It is continually changing and evolving to meet the needs and desires of tourists.

IMPACT OF HISTORICAL EVENTS ON TRAVEL

The travel industry is very sensitive to historical events. Thus, the horrible attack on the United States on September 11, 2001, by Islamic terrorists had a profound impact on travel, and it has taken approximately a year for the travel

Table 4.6. Growth of the Cruise Industry

Year	Number of Cruise Passengers
1970	500,000
1995	5,000,000
2001	9,800,000
2010	21,000,000 (estimated passengers)

Table 4.7. Categories of Cruise Lines

Category	Cruise Lines
Budget	Commodore, Fantasy, Regal
Contemporary	Carnival, Royal Caribbean, NCL
Premium	Princess, Holland America, Celebrity
Specialty	Windstar, Pearl, Orient
Luxury	Seabourn, Cunard, Silversea, Crystal

industry to recover. The horrific bombing of a nightclub in Bali in 2002 devastated tourism in Bali and Indonesia and has had a ripple effect all through Southeast Asia. Terrorist attacks, wars, fears of being robbed or kidnapped, and tourism do not mix well. Tourists may not mind an occasional mistake in their travel arrangements and an occasional inconvenience, but they do not want to endanger themselves. After the bombing in Bali, for example, hotel bookings in Bali dropped from 70 percent occupancy to 10 percent occupancy.

So tourism exerts a profound force on countries that want to develop the travel industry to make themselves safe for tourists and to become politically stable. A number of my friends who had planned to visit Egypt, for example, canceled their trips because they thought the country was too dangerous and that it was best, as they put it, "to steer clear of the Middle East." In the same light, the Intifada in Israel has had a devastating impact on tourism there. The same applies to many other countries where potential tourists are put off by anxiety about the instability of the country, the possibility of terrorist attacks, and their safety.

Neither its rhetoric or even the informational aspect of its discourse has a decisive effect on the buyer. What the individual does respond to, on the other hand, is advertising's underlying leitmotiv of protection and gratification, the intimation that its solicitations and attempts to persuade are the sign, indecipherable at the conscious level, that somewhere there is an agency (a social agency in the event, but one that refers directly to the image of the mother) which has taken upon itself to inform him of his own desires, and to foresee and rationalize these desires to his own satisfaction. He thus no more "believes" in advertising than the child believes in Father Christmas, but this in no way impeded his capacity to embrace an internalized infantile situation, and to act accordingly. Herein lies the very real effectiveness of advertising, founded on its obedience to a logic which, though not that of the conditioned reflex, is nonetheless very rigorous: a logic of belief and regression.

—*Jean Baudrillard*, The System of Objects

5

Travel Advertising: Images and Language

The travel industry advertises in media such as newspapers, magazines, television, and the Internet but mostly in travel magazines and in travel sections of newspapers, where it can find its target audiences more directly. The quotation from Baudrillard at the beginning of this chapter raises an interesting matter: most people believe they are not affected by advertising, which makes them all the more susceptible to being influenced by it. Does advertising work by suggesting solutions to us for problems we didn't know we had? Or by other means? Nobody is sure how advertising works, but we are all certain that when it does work it works on other people, not on us.

TOURIST ADVERTISING VERSUS TRANSPORTATION ADVERTISING

We need to make a distinction between advertising that is directly related to tourism, such as advertisements by foreign countries and travel destinations, and advertising related to travel, such as advertising by airlines. Airline advertising targets a form of transportation rather than being travel advertising, as I am using the term, but since tourists need to be transported from wherever they live to wherever they wish to go, this kind of advertising can be thought of as related to travel advertising but not tourism advertising. There is a great deal of automobile advertising and automobiles are used by people when they take trips, but I don't think we can reasonably describe automobile advertising as a kind of tourism advertising.

TRAVEL + LEISURE MAGAZINE ADVERTISING

If you look at the October 2002 issue of *Travel + Leisure* magazine you discover something interesting—a great deal of the advertising is not for products involved with travel. Table 5.1 lists the first ten one- or two-page advertisements in the issue.

Table 5.1.   Advertising in October 2002 issue of
***Travel + Leisure* Magazine**

Product	Size of Advertisement
Hummer automobile	Two-page spread
Faconnable (fashions)	Two-page spread
American Express	Two-page spread
IBM and Intel chips	Two-page spread
Rolex watches	One page
Mercedes-Benz	Two-page spread
Adrienne Vittadini	One page
Sprint	Two-page spread
Pebble Beach	One page
Epson printers, scanners	Two-page spread

You can see that only one travel advertisement appears in the first ten advertisements . . . and there is only one more travel advertisement in the next twenty pages. So it is obvious that much of the advertising in this magazine is directed at people who travel and who, advertisers assume, have the financial resources to purchase such products as Rolex watches and Mercedes-Benz automobiles—that is, people in the higher income brackets. Hotel advertisements appear on page 29 (Ritz-Carlton) and page 43 (W Hotels). We have to wait until page 49 for a real international travel advertisement—a two-page spread for the Adventure Collection:

> Where in the world do you want to go? . . . and who in the world should take you there?
> Introducing: Adventure Collection.
> Eight travel companies with over 200 years combined experience creating unforgettable journeys.

Looking at this issue of *Travel + Leisure* magazine, which is one of the more important travel magazines, we need to turn any number of pages before finding what I would describe as travel and tourism advertising. When we get to actual tourism advertising, as I define the term, we find the following full-page advertisements, excluding hotel advertisements and other auxiliary service advertisements such as credit cards (see table 5.2).

This issue had 288 pages, and the advertisements listed in table 5.2 were the only real full-page tourism advertisements in the magazine. Numerous advertisements promoted hotels, airlines, credit cards, fashions, perfumes, and

Table 5.2. **Full-Page Advertisements in October 2002** *Travel + Leisure*

Page	Travel Advertisement
57	Princess Cruises
65	Radisson Seven Seas Cruises
77	Crystal Cruises
81	Globus Tours
91	The Dominican Republic
93–94	Britain
99	Cunard Cruise Line
107	Norwegian Cruise Line
111–133	Special ad section on ski destinations in the United States
137	Silversea Cruise Line
147–149	Special ad section on cruise lines
153–154	Barbados
160–161	Holland America Cruise Line
165	Singapore
173	Arizona
174	Scottsdale, Arizona
195–218	Special ad section on Mexico
267–274	Special ad section on Hong Kong
275–278	Special ad section on New Mexico

other generally upscale products and services, but a rather limited number of tourism advertisements appeared. There were also quite a few "special advertising sections" in this issue, and some of those sections contained ads for hotels and other auxiliary services connected to travel and tourism.

KINDS OF TRAVEL ADVERTISING

We can see, then, that the magazine's touristic travel advertising, per se, falls into just a few categories: destination advertisements and cruise line "resort experience" advertisements. Cruise lines present a special case since, literally speaking, they are a form of transportation, but they also are connected to destinations—you take a cruise to visit certain places. And, for many travelers, the cruises are destinations in themselves.

So it seems reasonable to suggest, based on my analysis of this issue of *Travel + Leisure* magazine, that two basic categories of tourism and travel advertising really exist—destination advertisements, which represent the purest form of tourism advertising, and auxiliary travel advertisements, which involve all the other aspects of travel, such as transportation to destinations (airlines, buses, and railroads), accommodations (hotels, inns, bed and breakfast establishments), and other services that travelers and tourists use.

Simplifying to the extreme, we can say that tourists want to go places that differ from their own cultures and do things they think will be interesting and pleasurable. Some of the more common activities tourists seek involve various combinations of the following (taken from assorted advertisements):

Bicycling in foreign lands
Investigating foreign cultures
Going to places of great natural beauty such as rain forests
Having sea, sand, and surf experiences
Taking safaris
Sightseeing in places of historical interest
Hiking and trekking
Taking courses in everything from history to cooking
Playing golf

Tourists are in search of experiences and that which is different, and so destinations with rich and interesting cultures (that differ greatly from their own cultures) and destinations with great natural beauty are attractive to them, as long as they can feel secure and count on a decent amount of creature comforts. Some travelers prefer to stay in their tourist "bubbles" and more or less just observe and photograph places and people in other cultures, while other travelers try to enter into the cultures they visit and interact with natives and have experiences that they believe to be "authentic." They want to learn about these cultures as much as they can, given the amount of time at their disposal.

TRAVEL WRITING AS ADVERTISING

I have discussed travel advertising that announces itself as such—that is, advertising that deals, mostly, with foreign and in some cases exotic destinations. We've seen that most of the travel advertising in the issue of *Travel + Leisure* that I studied promoted destinations, though there was some advertising for support aspects of travel such as airlines and hotels. But there is another kind of advertising that is much more subtle. I am talking about the articles written by travel journalists describing the wonders of various destinations. On the cover of the magazine we find the following:

A headline for "The World's Best Spas"

A headline saying "Special Style Issue" and then listing the following places: Tuscany, Paris, London, Bangkok, Berlin, Arizona, New Zealand, Istanbul, Tokyo.

A headline reading "Diane and Tatiana von Furstenberg: Insider's Guide to L.A."

All of these headlines give readers a sense that these are very good places to go, and there is a kind of gilt (rather than guilt) by association by listing them all together. They all bask in the others' radiance.

I will deal with the way travel articles function as advertising by taking an example from *Travel + Leisure*—an article on Bangkok, which generally would be considered an exotic destination. The article, "Bangkok Modern," was written by Alan Brown (2002). The article has a headline, probably written by the editors of the magazine, that offers a glowing description of Bangkok:

> The air is cleaner, the traffic is better, and Thailand's capital is focused on the future, pulsing with energy and a sexy sense of design. Meet Asia's new metropolis of cool.

On the opposite page we find a full-page photo of a woman in a slinky black dress at "Q Bar, Bangkok's hippest nightspot, in the Sukhumvit neighborhood." Later, Brown meets an editor of the Thai edition of *Elle Decor* at a café run by the Greyhound chain in Thailand that "is the coolest place to hang out in."

Brown starts his article as follows:

> "So what's new in Bangkok?" I ask my friend Rungsima Kasikranund during a recent visit to Thailand's capital. "Spas, Latin dancing, and coffee bars," she replies offhandedly, as if to preclude any tiresome questions about good places for *pai thai* or upcoming festivals. Her answer—as well as her chic black outfit and the minimalist café in which we're sitting—tell me that Bangkok is, if not yet hip, then certainly on the cusp of hip.

Let's consider what this opening paragraph tells readers.

First, the article focuses on what's new in Bangkok, which suggests that there is reason for people who have visited the city before to return. Second, the author is talking with a friend, whose rather exotic name suggests she is Thai, which in turn suggests that he will be getting the inside dope from a savvy native who knows where to go and what to do. She replies that Bangkok now has "spas, Latin dancing and coffee bars," informing readers that there's a modern and international aspect to Bangkok they never knew existed. She wasn't going to answer Brown's question in the traditional way, about Bangkok food or festivals—an answer that might be of primary interest to backpackers or culture-seeking tourists. Third, she's dressed in a "chic black outfit" and they are in a "minimalist café," which tells us that we're getting information from a modern woman who can tell us about a different and "hip" kind of Bangkok than that described in traditional tourist brochures.

The article concludes with a fact sheet telling readers where to stay and where to eat and drink:

> Caledon. Many call this the city's best Thai restaurant, citing the serene atmosphere and beautiful dishes bursting with fresh flavors (and spices—not stinting on chiles here). Try the spicy shrimp appetizer and green curry. Dinner for two $42.

This article is no different from the other articles in the magazine about "cool" cities (Paris, London, Istanbul), sections of countries (Tuscany), states (Arizona), and countries (New Zealand) to visit. And the articles in this magazine are no different from those in other magazines, except that some travel magazines may be pitched to a more downscale reading audience and others to a more upscale one.

Restaurant reviews, theater reviews, and articles about cities and other destinations that we find in travel magazines and other travel publications provide information, but they also can be considered a form of advertising or, perhaps, public relations—similar in nature to the product placements we find in films, television shows, and now video games. And like many advertisements, the language is full of superlatives.

Many people who travel abroad buy travel guides that provide them with information about the places they are going. They also may read books about the places they will visit. Travel magazines offer more in-depth coverage and supposedly up-to-date information about certain tourist activities and destinations, but these articles tend to be quite formulaic and extremely enthusiastic about the places they describe.

There is also the irony that I've dealt with earlier—that many tourists want to go to places that are authentic and interesting and where there aren't *other* tourists. Readers of this magazine and other travel magazines, who are influenced by the articles they read, then tend to congregate in the various "hot," "hip," or "in" places, and turn them (if they weren't already) into widely visited tourist spots, where they can see all the other tourists who thought they were being "cool" or "hip" or "in the know" by going to these places.

LANGUAGE IN TRAVEL ADVERTISEMENTS: THE DISCOURSE OF DESIRE

Advertisements are a genre of communication that uses words and images to convince people exposed to the advertisement to purchase the product or service being promoted. In this section, I will discuss the linguistic aspects of advertising and in the next I will discuss the images found in advertising. The two work together, but I will separate them for analytical purposes.

When it comes to magazine advertising, the average reader glances at an advertisement for just a few seconds, generally speaking. Let me take the example of a couple with several weeks for their vacation who are trying to decide where to go. Readers who are interested in places to visit during their vacations will probably devote considerably more time to advertisements about travel destinations than other kinds of advertisements when they are thumbing through a travel magazine, since they are looking for information that will help them make up their minds about where they should go.

Copywriters for destinations are faced with the problem of convincing readers to visit "their" country or city or region. They make various appeals to their readers and try to strike a responsive chord in them. Copywriters may do this by making logical arguments, by using rhetorical devices, or by a combination of these methods. One device is to use associations that people will find positive and attractive. This technique is known, technically, as metonymy. The other is to use analogies that will affect readers, a device known as metaphor. A great deal of our thinking is metaphoric in nature, even though we may not recognize it. Metaphor and metonymy are techniques that build on a person's prior knowledge to make their points. Thus, for example, Rolls-Royce automobiles are associated with wealth and certain other characteristics, and copywriters who use Rolls-Royce know that their readers will interpret these automobiles in a certain way. In a kind of metonymy known as synecdoche, a part stands for a whole or vice versa. Thus, for example, a palm tree signifies "tropics, sun, and warm weather." So an image of a palm tree can be used to convey a great deal of information to people who are looking at advertisements. A weaker form of metaphor, known as a simile, uses "like" or "as." I explain these devices in table 5.3.

I will focus on two destination advertisements here—one for Honduras and another for Hungary. These advertisements are found in various issues of *Arthur Frommer's Budget Travel.*

An Advertisement for Honduras (November 2002)

Consider the language found in a full-page advertisement for Honduras. It shows a photograph of a woman in a bikini diving into a lake (or some other body of water). Above the photo we read "There's a world." On the side of the photograph reads:

> There's a land where you will learn the poetry of the wind through the rain forest, where the immense silence of its raw and untouched beauty will make you feel that time is no longer of consequence. Where you can learn the secrets of the forest. Honduras.

Underneath we find three small images—one is a map, another a Mayan head, and the third a scuba diver. Under these images we read "Tropical Nature," "Maya Renaissance," and "Caribbean Creation." Then underneath that:

Honduras
One small country, three wide worlds.

Table 5.3. Rhetorical Devices Used in Advertising

Metaphor	*Metonymy*
Analogy	Association
My love is a rose	Rolls-Royce suggests great wealth
Simile	*Synecdoche*
My life is *like* a rose	Palm tree = tropics

This copy uses metonymic associations we all have learned, in the course of growing up, about the magic of nature—in this case, rain forests—to spiritually enhance people by their quiet beauty.

Visitors to Honduras, it is asserted, will find a "raw" and "untouched" primitive wilderness, uncontaminated by civilization, where they will feel some kind of mystical communion with nature. This experience supposedly has the power to make people escape from "time," by which is meant their problems and other aspects of their everyday lives. They will learn the secrets of the forest. So travel is a learning experience, among other things, and what is learned is profound.

The style of the copy is pseudo-poetic and draws on the notion that reading poetry is somehow elevated and ennobling. This idea harks back, ultimately, to the romantic poets in England, who wrote so movingly about nature. This advertisement is directed at the segment of the traveling public that likes nature touring. But the three small images inform readers that in addition to being spiritually refreshed by the tropical nature of the rain forests, they can also explore Mayan ruins and enjoy the benefits of Caribbean lifestyle activities, such as scuba diving. Honduras, we are told, is a small country—which will make potential tourists feel they can thoroughly and easily explore it—and yet it has three worlds for tourists to experience.

An Advertisement for Hungary (September 2002)

I will consider one other destination advertisement—one for Hungary. It is a full-page advertisement on the right-hand side of a double page; on the left is a column full of copy. The advertisement is a hodgepodge of type styles and images and is not aesthetically pleasing.

The left-hand advertisement features a large, rather murky photo of people in a large indoor spa, with three small postage stamp–sized photos on the right-hand side of the page: one of a seascape and two with people in spas. The copy on this page reads:

> Open doors, open hearts, open minds:
> Hungary—Adventures for body and soul.
> Budapest Spa Special from $977 + Airport tax.
> 7 nights at a World Class Spa Resort blended in the rich
> culture of Budapest.* Call your Travel Agent or 1-800-448-4321.
> *more details on opposite page.

On the opposite page, in a two-inch column, we find the headline "Hungary has always been a hub and a meeting point in the very heart of Europe" and the following "sell":

> You can find here the footprints of the Barbarians, the Roman and Ottoman Empires. You can trace the early Catholicism as well as visit the largest operating synagogue in Europe. Full-fledged market economy and a unique blend of cultural, architectural, culinary and everyday lifestyles mark the whole country, particularly the beautiful capital city of Budapest.

After discussing Budapest's various cultural benefits, such as classical music, opera, gypsy music, museums, and restaurants, it concludes:

> The trip is invigorating for not only the soul but the body as well. You are spiritually and physically refreshed by the end of the tour after submerging in the great spa traditions of Hungary dating back to Roman and Turkish times and, at the same time, enjoying the rich cultural traditions and programs Budapest can offer. The Hungarian spa package is an offer you simply can't refuse!

Let's consider some of the language used in this advertisement. We find phrases such as "adventures for body and soul," "world class," and "rich culture," assuring readers intrigued by the idea of spending a week in Budapest that they would make a wise choice to do so. At the end of their vacation they will find themselves "spiritually and physically refreshed," suggesting that this vacation involves both their bodies and their souls. Taking advantage of the Budapest Spa Special, then, has spiritual dimensions of some magnitude and is good for one's soul as well as one's body.

Both the Honduras advertisement and the Hungary advertisement, which I chose randomly (looking for unconventional places), attempt to suggest that travel to their countries will be spiritually uplifting—in Honduras, in a tropical rain forest; in Hungary, in a course of spa treatments in a beautiful city with a rich cultural tradition. Both of these experiences, so different in what they offer, provide the same outcome: tourists will have adventures and they will find some kind of spiritual refreshment and enlightenment. They both build on a metaphor—travel is an adventure . . . that happens to be good for the soul.

Other aspects of travel may involve pleasure, such as scuba diving or going to the opera in Budapest, but ultimately travel and tourism involve more profound matters: a desire to experience wonderful things and to have profound experiences. Both of these advertisements—and advertising in general—play on desires people have to enrich their lives, to awaken their spiritual dimensions. The discussion that follows, of copy in a Lindblad brochure, shows how companies seek to play on our desire for unusual and spiritually elevating experiences.

Lindblad Expeditions

A recent Lindblad Expeditions catalog—Explorations: New Expeditions, Fresh Experiences, 2002–2003 offers an interesting insight into one of the problems tourist agencies face, namely finding something "new" and interesting to do. The Lindblad catalog explains:

> **Expeditionists, not tour guides**
>
> Once upon a not-too-distant time, the word "unexplored" applied to a good portion of the planet. It no longer does. But just because the planet's various pockets have all been located doesn't mean they've all been "picked." We take considerable satisfaction in knowing that the worlds—"remote," "pristine," "wild"—are incredibly rich, promissory and inviting. (Incidentally, each of these worlds seems to contain an implied "still." A reminder to us of the vital, ongoing need for conservation worldwide.) We head out each season full of the wonder of discovery—not to see what no one has ever seen, but to see what we haven't yet seen, to learn and to take what we learn back to enrich our personal understanding. . . . And that's why our voyages are expeditions, not cruises. Because they are active, not passive. (2003, 4)

Later on they mention that one of their voyagers said he went with Lindblad because he wanted to "experience" the places they go and not just passively observe them.

Lindblad argues that adventures are still possible and distances itself from ordinary tourism, which it describes as passive and based on observation and little else. The price for this "experiencing" is quite high; Lindblad charges considerably more for its "voyages" than cruise companies charge for cruises of the same number of days and nights. For example, a ten-night Lindblad expedition/cruise in Alaska starts at $3,690, while the same cruise with a conventional cruise line might start at $1,300 for a premium cruise line such as Princess cruises, which offers round-trip cruises from San Francisco. In its catalog, Lindblad argues that it is truly involved with ecotourism and promotes conservation while many other tourist companies claim to be involved in ecotourism but don't support conservation at all.

Lindblad Expeditions is an example of the segmentation found in the travel industry, where different companies provide the kind of experience tourists with certain interests are looking for. From its catalog, Lindblad seems to be a travel company that uses relatively small ships (around 100 passengers) for its cruises and is much more involved in visiting small and out-of-the-way places and fostering encounters with wildlife than the conventional cruise line. For example, Lindblad has cruises to Antarctica.

Lindblad plays on the romantic connotations of "expeditions" to differentiate itself from more conventional travel companies. Its catalog is full of maps and itineraries and says nothing about food or entertainment or the size of cabins. Lindblad, then, positions itself as a polar opposite—or should it be Antarctic south-polar opposite—of traditional cruise lines and travel companies.

IMAGES IN TRAVEL ADVERTISING: PICTORIAL DESIRE
The images found in advertisements play an important role in convincing people to purchase a product or a service. "Seeing is believing," and making it possible for people to see beautiful seascapes or interesting shots of cities enables viewers of advertisements to put themselves into the scene that is pictured and imagine—in their mind's eye—what being in a tropical rain forest or a spa in Budapest might be like.

Of course the images we find in advertisements are highly selective and chosen to emphasize positive aspects, in the case of travel advertising, of destinations. And talented photographers have the ability to capture marvelous images that enhance the copy in advertisements and contribute greatly to selling a destination.

The visual aspects of advertisements are important, as John Berger explains in his book *Ways of Seeing*:

> It is seeing which establishes our place in the surrounding world; we explain that world with words, but words can never undo the fact that we are surrounded by

it. . . . The way we see things is affected by what we know or what we believe."
(1972, 7–8)

Seeing, he adds, is "an act of choice." We don't just see everything but, in effect, choose what we want to look at, and when we do this, we are always thinking about the relationship that exists between what we see and our lives.
Berger defines an image as

> a sight which has been re-created or reproduced. It is an appearance, or a set of appearances, which has been detached from the place and time in which it first made its appearance and preserved—for a few moments or a few centuries. Every image embodies a way of seeing. Even a photograph. For photographs are not, as is often assumed, a mechanical record. Every time we look at a photograph, we are aware, however slightly, of the photographer selecting that sight from an infinity of other sights. (1972, 9–10)

So images are mediated, and the artist or photographer who creates an image always chooses to emphasize certain things and neglect others.

Technically speaking, an image is a collection of signs. A sign, as I explained in chapter 2, can be defined as anything that can be used to stand for something else. (Let us recall also that with signs, the relationship between signifiers and signifieds is arbitrary and based on convention.) We find meaning in the world, then, by learning what signs mean. We learn how to interpret signs from various sources such as our parents, our teachers, our friends, and, to a great degree, from the media and advertising.

Semioticians tell us that we continually send signs about ourselves to others and receive signs from others about themselves. For example, we "read" signs such as facial expressions, body language, body ornaments, eyeglasses styles, hair styles, and the clothes people wear to get information about them. When it comes to print advertisements, you can analyze words and language, colors, typefaces, and spatiality (amount of white space), all of which are signs that people interpret on the basis of their general fund of knowledge.

Let's consider photographs, the most common kind of image found in print advertising. If there are people in the advertisement, readers scrutinize them to get some sense of their social class, their personalities, and anything else they can find, and they do this by examining various signs such as those just discussed.

It is important to realize that images have the power to persuade. In his book *Visual Persuasion: The Role of Images in Advertising*, Paul Messaris points out that images can generate emotions in readers. Thus images might make us feel we simply *must* visit this or that historic city or a rain forest. Images help advertisers bypass any constraints that our logical faculties might want to impose on our decision making when it comes to spending money.

He adds something quite interesting. As a result of our biological evolution, scholars have suggested, people demonstrate certain hard-wired "response tendencies." That is, our response to certain images is not cultural but connected to our biological evolution. He offers the example of someone in an advertisement looking directly at the spectator, which "draws its attention getting power from our real-life tendency to look back when we are looked at" (1997, 4).

So, images of lush tropical rain forests, beaches with white sand and palm trees next to a blue ocean, wild animals, and little children in native costumes may have the power to evoke built-in responses on the part of readers. In addition, images may play on our desire to escape from our mundane everyday lives—if only for a short period of time—or to do the things that people we identify with (movie stars, well-known travelers) do. People often decide to visit places they see in movies or television shows. Images, then, can be powerful and maybe, in certain cases, even coercive.

APPEALS OF ADVERTISEMENTS

Advertisers need to take into account matters such as socioeconomic class, gender, age, values, taste levels, and lifestyles in their readers, which means that different travel magazines run different kinds of advertisements in them. You reach a different audience with *Travel + Leisure* than you do with *Arthur Frommer's Budget Travel*.

Table 5.4.   Appeals Found in Travel Advertisements

Appeal	Advertisement
Culture	Hungarian spas
Nature	Honduras
Historical sites	Hungarian spas
Culinary delights	Hungarian spas
Spiritual growth	Honduras, Hungarian spas
Luxury	Hungarian spas
New experiences	Honduras

The appeals of advertisements mirror, generally speaking, the appeals of travel. Some of the more common appeals in travel advertisements, based on the two advertisements discussed in this chapter, are found in table 5.4.

Travelers may be similar, generally speaking, in terms of wanting pleasurable and uplifting experiences, but there is a world of difference between how travelers try to satisfy their desires; some travelers are interested in budget travel and like to stay in small hotels and eat in small restaurants where the "locals" eat, while others like to stay in five-star luxury hotels and eat in very fancy and expensive restaurants. Some travelers like to go on guided tours while others like to rent a car and wander around some area, such as the south of France, stopping where they feel like it and spending as much time as they want wherever they want to spend it.

The ambiguity of the traveler's status, his "truth," creates a role and a function, reporting of a world that is assumed to contain all those strange and marvelous things, excluded by domestic reality that creates order through the repression of anomalies. The stranger is expected to be an anomaly, and to tell of those impossibilities that define an outer world.

Indeed, this becomes a convention within traditional travel literature: "[A]ny traveler's tale that claims to be a faithful report must contain a category of *Thoma* (marvels and curiosities). Travel literature long fulfilled the function of specifying alternative worlds, their reality at best problematical to those whose view of the world was limited by walls and channeled through gates. Seventeenth- and eighteenth-century travel writers were much disturbed by the traditional role of travelers as fictionalizers of the world and took great pains to establish a narrative style of descriptions, which we have come to know as nonfiction—a narrative of truths, observations, and facts.

—*Eric J. Leed*, The Mind of the Traveler: From Gilgamesh to Global Tourism

6

Travel Writing as an Art Form

Let's consider one of our earliest travel writers, Herodotus. Here is a selection from his description (c. 440 B.C.) of Egyptian culture:

> Concerning Egypt itself I shall extend my remarks to a great length, because there is no country that possesses so many wonders, nor any that has such a number of works which defy description. Not only is the climate different from that of the rest of the world, and the rivers unlike any other rivers, but the people also, in most of their manners and customs, exactly reverse the common practice of mankind. The women attend the markets and trade, while the men sit at home at the looms; and here, while the rest of the world works the woof up the warp, the Egyptians work it *down;* the women likewise carry burdens upon their shoulders, while the men carry them upon their heads. Women stand up to urinate, men sit down. They eat their food out of doors in the streets, but relieve themselves in their houses, giving as a reason that what is unseemly but necessary, ought to he done in secret, but what has nothing unseemly about it, should be done openly. A woman cannot serve the priestly office, either for god or goddess, but men are priests to both.
>
> . . . In other countries the priests have long hair, in Egypt their heads are shaven; elsewhere it is customary, in mourning, for near relations to cut their hair close; the Egyptians, who wear no hair at any other time, when they lose a relative, let their beards and the hair of their heads grow long. All other men pass their lives separate from animals, the Egyptians have animals always living with them; others make barley and wheat their food, it is a disgrace to do so in Egypt, where the grain they live on is spelt, which some call zea. Dough they knead with their feet, but they mix mud, and even take up dung with their hands.

What we find in Herodotus is what we find in many travel writers—a tendency to exaggerate, to look for the remarkable and exceptional, a fascination with those who do things differently from ourselves, a merging—at times—of fact and fiction. Early travel books were often quite fantastic. In modern times, as the Leed quotation that begins this chapter points out, travel writing has changed somewhat, but we still must be cautious with travel writers and realize that they always have a highly selective point of view.

We can make a distinction between travelers who write, writers who travel, and professional travel writers, though in some cases they merge together. Much of the best writing about travel is done by writers who happen to travel here and there and write about their experiences. They need to be differentiated from travelers who write about their travels, generally in their journals or on Internet chat sites, and professional travel writers, who write primarily for travelers and tourists.

WRITERS WHO TRAVEL, TRAVEL WRITERS, AND TRAVELERS WHO WRITE

Herodotus, an ancient historian, offers us a fascinating and fantastic portrait of the Egyptian life and culture, pointing out how different the Egyptians are from people in other lands. Egypt is a country, he writes, with many wonders and works that defy description, where the people are "the reverse" of the common practices of mankind.

Herodotus, like many writers in earlier days who traveled (from the ancient times until perhaps the twentieth century), writes about incredible things and "wonders" in the places he visited. It was not unusual for writers who traveled in those days to exaggerate or invent things that would astound their readers. Even today, in an era of mass media, many people have utterly ridiculous notions of what life in America is like, and many Americans probably have the same notions about what life in many other countries is like. What is important to realize is that travel writers shape people's notions about places and cultures, though not to the extent they did before the development of the mass media and the Internet.

There is a long tradition of wonderful travel writing from many writers and scholars, such as Ralph Waldo Emerson, Mark Twain, and Henry James from the United States; Charles Dickens, D. H. Lawrence, Robert Louis Stevenson, and Thomas Hardy from the United Kingdom; and Roland Barthes, Alexis de Tocqueville, and Claude Lévi-Strauss from France. These writers were not travel writers per se, but writers who wrote about places they had visited. Their focus, generally speaking, was on the culture and character of the people in the lands they visited.

TRAVELERS WHO WRITE ABOUT THEIR EXPERIENCES

Alexis de Tocqueville is an example of a traveler who writes about his experiences. He was only in the United States for nine months—from May 1831 to February 1832—yet his book *Democracy in America* is considered a classic and offers many brilliant insights into American political institutions, culture, and character that are still studied and analyzed and, in many cases, still correct.

De Tocqueville was, sociologically speaking, "a stranger" who was able to see things about American society and culture to which many Americans were blind. For example, his speculations about "individualism" in America—he coined the term—are still valid and one of the most cogent explanations of this phenomenon to this day.

Many travelers keep journals in which they write about the places they have visited and things they have done. With the popularity of the Internet, many travelers now write about their trips in various Internet chat rooms and in their blogs. If you surf the Internet, you can find an enormous amount of information written by travelers about hotels, restaurants, and places they have visited and cruises they have taken. This kind of writing, generally by amateurs, may not have much literary quality, but it can provide information to those considering visiting a country or region or city who are looking for good hotels and restaurants and are curious about what there is to see and do in the sites they intend to visit.

PROFESSIONAL TRAVEL WRITERS AND
THE CONVENTIONS OF TRAVEL WRITING

It is professional travel writers that I wish to discuss here—writers who recount their travels and adventures—not writers of guidebooks, though they are also professional travel writers. I have read a number of books by such writers as Jan Morris (widely considered to be the dean of contemporary travel writers), Pico Iyer, Paul Theroux, and Colin Thubron; it is their work that I will use in this discussion of the conventions of travel writing. I will use the term *travel writing* to cover the kind of writing done by authors such as these.

Travel writing is a literary genre, and like all genres, it has certain conventions that it follows (i.e., it is formulaic). Some of the conventions of professional travel writing are discussed in this chapter. They may not always be followed, but they are typical of most writing by professional travel writers.

TRAVEL WRITING AS AUTOBIOGRAPHY

Travel writing is generally written in the first person and is autobiographical in nature in the sense that travel writers offer their readers a record of their adventures and observations. What makes travel writers popular is the quality of their prose and their ability to describe fascinating adventures and interesting encounters with individuals. Readers can empathize with the writer and have "virtual" travel experiences of their own. In many cases, travel writers write about their encounters with other travelers, who often have interesting eccentricities and strange ideas.

Consider, for example, what Colin Thubron writes in the beginning of his book *In Siberia*:

> I am sliding out of European Russia into somewhere which seems less a country than a region in people's minds, and even at this last moment, everything ahead—the violences of geography and time—feels a little thinned, too cold or vast to be precisely real. The place from which you will not return.
>
> I chose it against my will. I was subverted by the sudden falling open of a vast area of the forbidden world. The immensity of Siberia had shadowed all my Asian journeys. So the casual beginnings—the furtive glance in an atlas—began to nag and deepen, until the wilderness seemed less to be empty than overlooked, or scrawled with invisible ink. Insidiously, it began to infect me. (1999, 2)

Siberia had, it seems, always fascinated Thubron, but foreigners had been limited for many years to only five towns in Siberia, at various places along the Trans-Siberian Railway. And then suddenly, Siberia, a "forbidden" world, was opened up and Thubron could not resist going there.

Without stretching credulity too much, we can consider the books that travel writers publish as parts of their ongoing autobiographies. All writing reveals a great deal about the author, but travel writing is a genre in which an author's opinions and values are unusually evident. It is not too far-fetched, then, to see travel writing as having this autobiographical element, in which the author's interests and passions are there for all to see. We are seeking information about people and places when we read travel writers, but we also must become captivated by the personality, taste, and authorial "voice" of the travel writer.

TRAVEL WRITERS HAVE A POINT OF VIEW

Travel writing always has a point of view—that of the author, who focuses attention on certain things and neglects others. That is, travel writing is always mediated by the consciousness of the writer. (Travel writing is not reportage, and even reportage is selective and mediated by what a reporter thinks is important.) Some writers tend to be rather cynical—distrustful of the people they meet in their travels and somewhat negative about human nature. These writers tend to focus on that which is nasty and unpleasant in the places they go—and this is reflected in their work. Other travel writers are much more sympathetic and more likely to find positive things to write about. We must recognize that travel writing is a form of criticism, not unlike film, theater, and restaurant reviews, in which the sensibility and taste of the author is of great importance.

HYPERDETAIL AS A STYLISTIC DEVICE OF TRAVEL WRITERS

Travel writing is very descriptive, generally full of detailed portraits of places and people encountered by the traveler. Our example from Herodotus is full of details about the curious customs of the Egyptians. One way travel writers achieve their effects is to offer very detailed verbal portraits that generate images in our minds about what a particular place is like and what the people who live there are like.

Consider Pico Iyer's description of Saigon in his chapter "Yesterday Once More" from his book *Falling Off the Map: Some Lonely Places of the World*:

> One evening I counted more than a hundred two-wheel vehicles racing past me in the space of sixty seconds, speeding round the jam-packed streets as if on some crazy merry-go-round, a mad carnival without a ringmaster. I walked into a dance club and found myself in the midst of a crowded floor of hip gay boys in sleeveless T-shirts doing the latest moves to David Byrne; outside again, I was back inside the generic Asian swirl, walking through tunnels of whispers and hisses. "You want boom-boom?" "Souvenir for your dah-ling?" "Why you not take special massage?" Shortly before midnight, the taxi girls stream out of their nightclubs in their party dresses and park their scooters outside the hotels along "Simultaneous Uprising" Street. Inside, Indian and Malaysian and Japanese trade-fair delegates huddle in clusters circling like excited schoolboys and checking out the mini-skirted wares, while out on the street legless beggars hop about, and crippled girls offer oral services, and boys of every stripe mutter bargains for their sisters. (1993, 134–135)

Iyer's description of Saigon is remarkable for its detail and sense of excitement. You get the sense, from the language he uses and the scene he describes, that Saigon is just throbbing with energy and is a fabulous, out-of-this-world—that is, wild—kind of place. He suggests that Saigon is very wild and then backs up this characterization with a great deal of detailed evidence. Notice, also, how much of this passage has to do with human sexuality.

Saigon comes off—at least as Iyer describes it—as a place where any and every sexual desire can be accommodated. I've visited Saigon (its official name is Ho Chi Minh City), and while it is frenetic, I didn't see the kind of scenes he described. It no doubt exists, but it is only one aspect of Saigon that Iyer chose to focus on, . . . not the quiet, restaurant-lined alleys and main streets I visited when I was there.

His evocation of Hanoi is equally graphic and suggests the power of globalization and the mass media, a subject he deals with in a later book. He discusses the "cash-register quickness and low-key patriotism" of the Vietnamese, who are more interested in making money than in political ideology:

> the nominal principles of the Party are contradicted all day long by a cacophony of deals. Everywhere seems a marketplace in Hanoi, and every street is bubbling over with free trade: one block given over to a stack of black-and-white TVs, one to a rack of bicycles. In another block, thirty barbers were lined up, with their backs to traffic, their mirrors set along the wall before them. Old men puffed Hero and Gallantes cigarettes over pyramids of Nescafe bottles, bookshops exploded with stacks of Madonna fan mags, copies of *Ba Tuoc Mongto Crixto* (and, of course, piles of TOEFL Preparation Books). In the covered market, fifteen-dollar a kilo turtles and fat snakes sat next to MARADONA JEANS caps and shirts with ONE HUNDRED DOLLARS on them. (1993, 122–123)

Notice the amount of detail Iyer incorporates into his description and how he focuses only on certain aspects of life in these cities. He loves lists and brand names, and he piles on one detail after another, generating a kind of breathless sense of wonder about these cities. Iyer offers an exciting image of certain sections of these cities and what goes on in them; it is important to consider what he focuses his attention on and to consider, as is the case in all travel writing, what he neglects.

THE QUASI-FICTIVE NATURE OF TRAVEL WRITING

Like fiction, travel writing devotes a great deal of attention to the adventures of the travel writers and to the characters they meet. In some cases, travel writers devote more time to character sketches than to the places they are visiting.

It's instructive to look at the table of contents of Paul Theroux's *To the Ends of the Earth*—a collection of what he considers to be his best travel writing. The first set of selections comes from his book *The Great Railway Bazaar*:

The Mysterious Mr. Duffill

Looking out the Window in Yugoslavia

Dusk in Central Turkey

Sadik

Peshawar

The Village in the Railway Station

In Jaipur with Mr. Gopal

The Grand Trunk Express to the Real India

"I Find You English Girl"—Madras

Mr. Wong the Tooth Mechanic

Mr. Chatterjee's Calcutta

The Hopping Man

Memories of the Raj—Mr. Bernard in Burma

Gokreik Viaduct

The Hue-Danang Passenger Train, Vietnam 1973

The Trans-Siberian Express

You can see from this list the importance Theroux gives to the various interesting individuals he met in the course of his travels. And some of the other selections also focus on individuals, even though the title of the selection doesn't indicate that this is the case.

The fact that Theroux is also a novelist may explain the role that individuals, or is it more accurate to say *characters*, play in his books. In a sense, Theroux is writing what might be described as a kind of new-journalism hybrid "reality" novel describing his adventures with real people instead of portraying the adventures of imagined characters.

A blurb on the back cover of Colin Thubron's *In Siberia* is of interest in this respect. Richard Kapuscinski, author of *Imperium*, writes the following:

> A fascinating book! Once again, Colin Thubron has proved his mastery, his unique talent for reaching exceptional places and extraordinary people. Thanks to him we encounter a world which, in its beauty and awe, exceeds our imagination.

Thubron, like Theroux and other first-class travel writers, has a knack for finding the right places to go and, of equal importance, finding—or searching out—the right people to write about in his books. It's interesting to note that Jan Morris has also written a very fine novel, one that reads like a travel book, except that the adventures of the narrator and the people the narrator interacts with are all invented by Morris.

What makes the best travel writing so powerful is that it uses the conventions of fiction writing so superbly. Fiction involves made-up characters who have complicated relationships with other characters, who do various things, leading to some kind of a resolution and conclusion, . . . all of which evokes emotions in readers. We get the same thing from the best travel writers. They are able to interest us because of the quality of their prose, because of the insights they provide about the places they visit—frequently going beneath the surface to reveal important matters relating to social, economic, and political life—and because of the remarkable characters with whom they interact.

Good writers, whatever their genre, work a kind of magic on their readers, and the magic of travel writers involves helping readers gain insights into what might be described as the human condition and, in addition, a sense of empathy with people everywhere.

TRAVEL WRITING AS POP ANTHROPOLOGY AND POP SOCIOLOGY

One thing that travel writers try to do is give readers a sense of what everyday life is like in the places they visit. That is, travel writing, even though it may focus a great deal of attention on individuals, is always concerned with the society and culture of the place visited. Writers use the individuals they describe as a means of giving insights into the places where these individuals live.

The very detailed lists of objects that Iyer mentions and his description of the scenes he sees, with the barbers lined up with their mirrors and so on, are meant to give readers an insight into the nature of life in these two cities, and of Vietnam in general. Consider his evocation of Iceland in his chapter "Rock n' Roll Ghost Town":

> I knew, before I visited, a little of the epidemic oddness of the place: there was no beer in Iceland in 1987, and no television Thursdays; there was almost no trees, and no vegetables. Iceland is an ungodly wasteland of volcanoes and tundra and Geysir, the mother of all geysers, a country so lunar that NASA astronauts did their training here; a place of fumaroles and softataras, with more hot springs and mud pools and steam holes than any other wilderness on earth. . . . Even "civilization" seems to offer no purchase for the mind here: nothing quite makes sense. . . . Roughly three eldest children in every four are illegitimate here, and because every son of Kristjan is called Kristjansson and every daughter Krisjandottir, mothers always have different surnames from their children (and in any case are rarely living with the fathers). (1993, 67)

Iyer is able to give us a fascinating portrait of Iceland in this passage, which reads like something one might get from a sociologist, offering readers remarkable insights into Icelandic landscape, character, and culture. Iyer describes the women there as "honey cheeked beauty queens" and the men as "hatchet-faced yahoos," suggesting a sense of incredulity that such beautiful women would find such unattractive and unsympathetic men appealing or sadness that these beautiful women had such limited options.

NARRATIVE ASPECTS OF TRAVEL WRITING

In keeping with its fictive nature, travel writing generally has a strong narrative line. It isn't possible to demonstrate this in short selections that I might quote, but the best travel writers tell stories that interest and entertain us. Travel writers seek out adventures and interesting personalities to write about, and the journeys travel writers take usually have a beginning, a series of adventures, and some kind of conclusion.

Consider, for example, Jan Morris's chapter on Hong Kong, "Anglo-China," in her book *Travels*. She starts her chapter as follows:

> A foreign devil of my acquaintance, on my first morning in Hong Kong, took me to the top of an exceedingly high mountain, by funicular, from Garden Road, and invited me to worship.

The kingdoms of the world lay before us. The skyscrapers of Victoria, jam-packed at the foot of the hill, seemed to vibrate with pride, greed, energy and success, and all among them the traffic swirled and the crowds milled and the shops glittered, and the money rang. Beyond lay the ships in their hundreds, like a fast fleet anchored in the roadsteads from Chai Wan to Stonecutter's Islands, here a super-tanker, here a cruise ship, there a warship all a'bristle, with their attendant sampans busy beside them, and the junks and tugs and pilot boats hurrying everywhere, and the hydrofoil foaming off to Macao, and the ceaseless passage of the Star ferries backwards and forwards across the harbour. (1976, 92–93)

Here, Morris offers a wonderful portrait of the city and gives readers a sense of its spirited and animated energy. Then she moves on to more descriptions of the city, a discussion of Hong Kong's "Chineseness," thoughts about its dehumanized aspects, speculations on the lives of the British in Hong Kong and about politics in Hong Kong, considerations about the striking social contrasts she observes, descriptions of various places she visits, and ruminations about all sorts of things related to Hong Kong's politics and social life. She possesses a superb ability to seamlessly blend together social commentary, description, and characterizations of people and places, and so her readers are both entertained and educated at the same time.

Morris concludes this chapter with a visit to Lok Ma Chau, on the Chinese frontier:

It was a lovely day when I was there, and the view seemed almost complementary to the prospect my friend had offered me, two weeks before, looking over Hong Kong harbour from the top of the funicular. If that view was all punch, this was all pull. There across the river lay a silent country, green, blue, and mauve—green for the paddy-fields that stained the wide plain, blue for the sheets of water that lay mirror-like beneath the sky, mauve for the hills of the horizon. China! It struck me not so much as peaceful or serene, as *simple*—innocent, perhaps. It looked like a world stripped of its pretensions and complexities, and as I stood there in the sunshine thinking about it for the first time I felt a stir of that yearning within myself, and found myself looking towards China as though that silent landscape were calling me home.

Home to where? Home to what? As I wandered down the track towards my car, one of the stall-sellers spoke to me quietly, without urgency, across his wares. "Why don't you buy," he inquired, as though he genuinely, if mildly, wanted to the know the answer, "the thought of Chairman Mao?"—and he held up a small red book, bound in plastic.

"Get thee behind me," I said. (1976, 111)

Just like a fiction writer, Morris has a beginning and a resolution to her article, and the resolution draws on the beginning of the piece. "Get thee behind me," she says, alluding to the conclusion of that famous line, "Satan!"

Morris starts her article at one tourist site and ends at a different one, one that suddenly evokes in her a certain yearning for home—though, at the time she wrote this, she couldn't or wouldn't tell her readers where her home was or what it was like. She is Welsh and has in recent years settled in Wales in a new house, which she describes lovingly in a little book she wrote about the matter.

ANTHROPOLOGISTS AS TRAVEL WRITERS: LÉVI-STRAUSS

Claude Lévi-Strauss is the author of a classic book, *Tristes Tropiques: An Anthropological Study of Primitive Societies in Brazil,* the story of his research in Brazil, among other things. It was published in French in 1955 and in an English translation in 1970. Lévi-Strauss was, without question, one of the most influential anthropologists in the last fifty years of the twentieth century, and many would argue he was the most influential anthropologist during this period.

Nominally *Tristes Tropiques* is a social science work about various tribes in Brazil that Lévi-Strauss studied, but it is also a classic travel book, devoted to his travels to Brazil and throughout Brazil. In addition to these aspects, it offers many thoughts about the nature of travel. I will offer some passages about this aspect of the book, which is of most interest to us. It turns out that *Tristes Tropiques'* very first sentence is about travel:

> Travel and travellers are two things I loathe—and yet here I am, all set to tell the story of my expeditions. But at least I've taken a long while to make up my mind to it: fifteen years have passed since I left Brazil for the last time and often, during those years, I've planned to write this book, but I've always been held back by a sort of shame and disgust. (1970, 17)

He points out that it is not unusual for an anthropologist to spend weeks or months in order to get an interview with an informant, but what readers want is a raking over of his memory's "trash cans."

Lévi-Strauss laments the degree to which travel books have become popular and the soporific effects they have on readers:

> Amazonia, Africa, and Tibet have invaded all our bookstalls. Travel-books, expeditionary records, and photograph-albums abound; and as they are written or compiled with an eye mainly for effect the reader has no means of estimating their value. His critical sense once lulled to sleep, he asks only to be given "more of the same" and ends up devouring it in unlimited quantity. (1970, 17–18)

He is bothered that large numbers of people like the kind of books travel writers produce; the claim to fame of travel writers, he suggests perhaps unfairly, is that they have done a great deal of traveling and what they do is create unreal stereotypes to satisfy the desires of their readers. Yet he understands, he tells us, why people like travel books—because they preserve the illusion of a past that no longer exists and of differences between people that have been destroyed by what he calls a "mono-culture."

Humanity, he asserts, is preparing to produce civilization en masse as if it were a kind of sugar beet, and he longs for the days when one could really travel and see new things.

Like many travelers, Lévi-Strauss is concerned about the authentic, about what life was like before civilization's ineluctable march "of progress" corrupted and contaminated everyone everywhere. His conclusion is that we face a dilemma: either one travels in ancient times when much that one would see would be unintelligible or one travels in the present day, searching in vain for a vanished reality. In either case, he laments, he is the loser.

Let me add to this discussion of Lévi-Strauss's thoughts on travel one rather pessimistic selection:

> There was a time when travel confronted the traveller with civilizations radically different from his own. It was their strangeness, above all, which impressed him. But these opportunities have been getting rarer and rarer for a very long time. Be it in India or in America, the traveller of our day finds things more familiar than he will admit. The aims and itineraries which we devise for ourselves are above all, ways of being free to choose at what date we shall penetrate a given society. . . . The search for the exotic will always bring us back to the same conclusion, but we can choose between an early or a late stage of its development.

> The traveller becomes a kind of dealer in antiques—one who, having given up his gallery of primitive art for lack of stock, falls back on fusty souvenirs brought back from the flea-markets of the inhabited world. (1970, 90–91)

This image that Lévi-Strauss leaves us with—of travelers having to content themselves with junk bought at a flea market because there's no more primitive art (and exotic cultures) available, is a powerful one.

In this discussion of *Tristes Tropiques,* I focused my attention on Lévi-Strauss's speculations on travel. His book is a fabulous travel book, with long and marvelous descriptions of his explorations and investigations in various places in Brazil and his encounters with different tribes. Reading it reminded me of books I had read about explorers in Africa in the nineteenth century and early years of the twentieth century. Travelers truly were strangers in strange lands in those days.

Lévi-Strauss ends *Tristes Tropiques* with a beautifully written and poetic passage:

> Farewell to savages, then, farewell to journeying! And instead, during the brief intervals when humanity can bear to interrupt its hive-like labours, let us grasp the essence of what our species has been and still is, beyond thought and beneath society: an essence that may be vouchsafed to us in a mineral more beautiful than any work of Man: in the scent, more subtly evoked than our books, that lingers in the heart of a lily; or in the wink of an eye, heavy with patience, serenity, and mutual forgiveness, that sometimes, through an involuntary understanding, one can exchange with a cat. (1970, 398)

With that lament for the end of his traveling and expression of his hopes for humanity, Lévi-Strauss concludes his remarkable book. He searched through the dense jungles of Brazil for tribes that would enable him to understand the essence of human society by finding its most elemental forms and produced a work that is both a classic of anthropological research and of travel writing.

Tourism, so internationally commonplace for the postmodern scholar, has always been inseparable from shopping, sometimes called collecting. Florence might be seen as an open-air mall, with hundreds of shops and art sites, alternating art (which no one can afford) and fashion (which we can buy). Do we see the Ponte Vecchio and history or the glitter of gold in the many jewelry displays on that old covered bridge? Or are these inextricable, with tourism as historical, meaningful shopping? That the Kremlin is located just opposite the world's largest covered mall, the GUM department store, is ironic for the USSR, its political system failing in consumption. GUM has few items to buy, and those available are massively repetitious, sold in stalls as at a country fair. In addition, there are stores where only tourists can shop, revealing a double shopping standard. The relationship between the conclusion of the Cold War and international shopping is perhaps not as trivial as it might seem.

—*Patricia Mellencamp,* High Anxiety: Catastrophe, Scandal, Age, & Comedy

7

The Impact of Tourism

Certain mass communication theorists have argued that first world countries, such as the United States and Britain, are exporting their cultural values and lifestyles (especially as they relate to free enterprise capitalism and consumer cultures) to third world countries and imposing these values and lifestyles on them. This is done by the films and television shows the first world countries make and export to the third world countries. I will discuss this theory as it relates to tourism and, among other things, tourism's global aspects and economic impact.

TOURISM AND CULTURAL IMPERIALISM

The values and beliefs held by the writers of films and television shows are reflected in their works; the material is not propaganda and is not inserted into the various texts consciously, but nevertheless the impact of films, television shows, and other media such as books is great. This theory of cultural imperialism is also known as the "Coca-colonization" theory, reflecting the ubiquitous presence of Coca-Cola, as a symbol of American culture—all over the world.

In an analogous way, tourism also functions as a means of cultural imperialism. Tourists impose, to a certain degree, their values and beliefs—and, in particular, their desires—on foreign cultures. Tourists want to be comfortable, so suitable hotels need to be built. Tourists want to travel around the countries they visit, so roads and railroads and airports must be built. Tourists seek cultural experiences, so—in many cases—inauthentic native dances, musical exhibitions, and other kinds of theatrical works are created to cater to their tastes. It isn't always the case that traditional cultural forms of expression are watered down, modified, and made more palatable for tourists, but this happens a great deal.

The argument of the cultural imperialists is that eventually third world cultures, which are held to be fragile, are often overwhelmed and destroyed by first world cultures. This leads to a universal monoculture of the kind described by Lévi-Strauss in the previous chapter, in which cultures all over the world lose their distinctiveness and they all start resembling one another, with the United States being the ultimate model. For some theorists, mass tourism is the stage that comes after colonialism and is a kind of diffused and disguised imperialism.

There is good reason to dispute this hypothesis. As far as mass media are concerned, scholars have analyzed the way people in different countries interpret American television programs and find that they tend to impose their native belief systems and values on what they see. And my own travels have suggested to me that people in third world countries adapt first world institutions for their own purposes. For example, though there may be a few McDonald's restaurants in Marrakech, you don't get the feeling that American culture has "McDonaldized" Morocco. Curiously enough, an informant in Morocco told me that McDonald's has become a gathering place for women, since they aren't welcomed in coffee shops and traditional gathering places, in which you never see women. The Moroccans have adapted an American institution and are using it for their own purposes.

I would suggest that this is typical of what happens in third world countries when it comes to tourism. That is, people in the third world absorb various aspects of the first world—whether it is McDonald's hamburger restaurants or tourists—and make various adaptations and create new cultural forms to suit their needs. Cultures are always modifying themselves as they are exposed to new ideas and new things. This happens in the United States, as well, where the Italian espresso (and other coffee drinks based on it), as interpreted by Starbucks and other similar coffee shops, is now becoming very popular.

GLOBAL ASPECTS OF TOURISM

The fact that tourism is now a global phenomenon means that its impact is widespread, though its impact has varying effects in different countries. Globalism is also connected to modernization and the spread of values and institutions connected with this phenomenon. Tourists generally demand a certain level of comfort, which leads to the development of what might be described as a tourist-based infrastructure—hotels, restaurants, nightclubs, cultural centers, roads, access to airports and railroad systems, and so on—all the things that facilitate tourism. Of course, some tourists seek "nature" and are categorized as "adventure" tourists; they don't require, or want, the kind of hotels and other institutions that ordinary tourists want.

In his book *Tourism and Modernity: A Sociological Analysis*, Ning Wang discusses the impact that globalization has had on cultures:

> Globalization does not eradicate difference, variety, and diversity. Historically, the Enlightenment thinkers insisted that globalization, as the extension of Western order, reason, values, and civilization to the rest of the world, should lead to the universalization, homogenization, and Westernization of the world. History has proved that this was not only a justification of colonialism, but also a utopia. In reality, even if globalization has indeed led to what Hannerz (1987) calls "cultural creolization," it has not eradicated difference. Rather, difference is alive and well. The world today is one of difference, diversity, and pluralism rather than sameness. (2000, 133)

What has happened, Wang explains, is that we now have increased access to all the corners of the world, turning the world into something like the global village that Marshall McLuhan wrote about. As a result of the development of the airline industry and technological improvements in jet airliners, it is possible to reach anyplace in the world in a relatively short period of time and at relatively little expense, in many cases. But we don't travel long distances to go to places like our hometowns, so tourism, it can be suggested, requires difference and thus acts as a force for the maintenance of different and distinctive cultures and lifestyles.

You can purchase a ticket that allows you to travel all over the world for $1,200 or so. For example, the Sunday *San Francisco Chronicle* travel section always includes a half page of ads under the listing "World Travel Agents." One agency (www.JustFares.com) runs an advertisement with various world tours you can arrange. For $849 you can go to the following places from San Francisco: Hong Kong, Bangkok, Singapore, Bali, and back to San Francisco. For $1,299 you can go to the following places from San Francisco: Moscow, Delhi, overland to Peking, Los Angeles. For $1,399 you can take the following trip: Saigon, overland to Bangkok, Bali, Sydney, Auckland, Fiji, Los Angeles. My point is, for those who wish to travel and have the time and money, the world is now everyone's "oyster." In the course of my travels I've met quite a few people who have taken a year off from work to see the world.

Tourism now has a global reach, and the postmodern stylistic eclectic sensibility reflected in Jean-François Lyotard's *The Postmodern Condition* is an example of that. I quoted him in chapter 2 about eating a McDonald's hamburger for lunch and local cuisine for dinner, wearing Paris perfume in Tokyo and "retro" clothes in Hong Kong. What seems to have happened is that, ironically, rather than American (and one could add other first world countries here) culture wiping out all the other cultures, people all over the world—in the best postmodern manner—have put together a pastiche of different cultures in creating their individual lifestyles.

In Paris a French person might wear American blue jeans, have a cappuccino and a croissant for breakfast, visit the Louvre (and see the beautiful glass pyramid created by Chinese-American architect I. M. Pei), dine on Vietnamese food for lunch and Japanese food for dinner, see a German ballet company that evening, and, late at night, enjoy a Scotch at a bar and listen to jazz. And nowadays the same kind of thing happens all over the world.

MONOCULTURE VERSUS A MULTICULTURAL WORLD

The term *monoculture*, let me repeat, refers to the belief of some cultural theorists that the global reach of tourism and the impact of first world cultures—especially American culture—on third world ones will eventually result in every place in the world being similar to every other place. That is, we will eventually share one culture, and that culture will be very similar, in nature, to what you find in the United States.

One thing this theory assumes is that the United States is, more or less, all the same. But the fast food restaurants and malls that may be ubiquitous in America are only part of the picture. There are incredible differences between the landscapes and cultures of our gigantic urban centers, medium-sized cities, and small towns and between various regions in the United States. In fact, very important regional differences exist in America, such as between New England, the deep South, the Midwest, the West, the Pacific Northwest, the East Coast, and so on. These differences are reflected in the diverse architectural styles, dialects, cuisines, and ethnic groups found in these areas.

So even if the United States became the model for a world monoculture, you still would find a great deal of diversity in this monoculture. People make a mistake when they assume that the relative uniformity of certain aspects of American culture, such as our popular culture, upscale shopping streets, fast food restaurants, and malls, reflects a national uniformity.

Claude Lévi-Strauss feared that the age of true exploration was over and that the modern world was becoming a monoculture; I would suggest that the impact of tourism has been to modify certain aspects of cultures everywhere, but these adaptations often tend to help people preserve their cultures. Ironically, rather than the world becoming one monoculture, it seems to be moving in the other direction, and some countries, such as Canada and Iraq, seem to be in danger of breaking up into smaller countries as a result of a combination of religious, racial, ethnic, and linguistic differences.

THE ECONOMIC IMPACT OF TOURISM

When tourists visit a site of interest, unless they are just on a quick day visit or on a cruise, they need some kind of lodging, such as hotels or bed and breakfasts. Tourists of all kinds do a great deal of shopping—they often buy souvenirs, clothes, "native" artwork, and many other things. Shopping is a central element of tourism for many people, who sometimes go to certain places (Hong Kong, for example) specifically to buy certain things. Thus, Mellencamp's suggestion that the lack of good shopping brought down the Russian communist government and led to the end of the Cold War is quite reasonable. People behind the Iron Curtain could see (on television and in films) what other people had in their houses and wanted the various products that represent the "good life."

In addition, tourists often dine at local restaurants and take cabs or other forms of transportation to places they want to go for entertainment or other reasons. We can see, then, that tourism has a considerable economic impact in that it generates employment—it takes workers to keep hotels going, to cook and serve meals, to sell things in stores, and to drive cabs and buses. In addition to the jobs it creates, it provides foreign exchange and tax revenues. So there's an obvious economic impact to tourism.

Sites that want to attract tourists must develop their infrastructures in order to accommodate them in the manner they desire, so there are also costs connected to tourism. These costs, though perhaps *investments* is a better word, involve such things as building hotels, roads, and golf courses as well as developing cultural institutions such as museums and concert halls and supporting events of interest to various kinds of tourists (e.g., sports contests, rock concerts, and folk cultural exhibitions).

According to the World Tourism Organization, in 1997 there were close to 613 million tourist arrivals in sites of one kind or another. This statistic shows that a large number of people are going places. Economists use the term *multiplier effect* to describe the impact of money spent by tourists as it circulates through a site's economy (a city, region of a country, or the country as a whole). If there are strong links between different elements in the places where tourists visit—if companies involved with tourists hire local people to do various jobs and purchase food grown by local farmers—then the multiplier effect can be seen to be strong.

Money spent by tourists circulates to various groups in the places visited and enables the country where the tourists spend their money to purchase goods and services from the United States, thus effecting the balance of payments here. The negative aspect of tourism is that it generates a certain amount of inflationary pressure on the places where it flourishes and other pressures, such as on nature and natural resources.

TOURISM AND THE DESTRUCTION OF NATURE

One problem connected with tourism involves the destruction of nature or, in other cases, the modification of nature to suit the needs of tourism. For example, in Bali, so much agricultural land has been used for building hotels, restaurants, and roads that Bali is no longer self-sufficient in rice and must import it. The terrible explosion in a nightclub in 2002 devastated the tourism industry there, and for a while, without the ability to grow enough food, Bali experienced many problems. There were predictions of widespread hunger on the island if the tourists didn't return. Fortunately, they have returned, and Bali is once again a popular tourism site.

There is also the matter of the wear and tear inflicted by tourists on nature— even if they are sensitive to the fragility of nature. Some popular natural tourist sites are becoming ruined or "over-touristed," and in many cases governments need to limit access to such sites. Also, local developers often wish to build roads and buildings or make major changes in the natural ecology to satisfy tourists, which causes other problems.

On the other side of this coin, many countries have begun to realize that their natural sites of beauty are valuable resources that attract tourists, so it makes economic sense to maintain and improve these sites. So one positive by-product of tourism involves the preservation of places of natural beauty since they are valuable as tourist magnets. If you cut down all the trees in a rain forest, you can sell the lumber, but after that, the land doesn't make money. If you preserve a rain forest and tourists come to visit it, it keeps generating income. Tourism can therefore be a positive force when it comes to nature, and it isn't always the case that tourism's impact is negative.

PRESERVING OLD TOWNS AND HISTORICAL AREAS

In the same light, cities have discovered that it makes sense to preserve old towns and other historically important sites instead of bulldozing them and building things like condominiums and shopping malls. These "old town" areas possess interesting architecture and charm, and many of these sites in the United States that escaped the bulldozers have been turned into tourist attractions, full of restaurants and shops.

Old towns and quaint villages offer tourists an opportunity to step back in history, so to speak, and get a sense of what life might have been like a hundred years ago or so, when these townships were built up. They are visually different from modern settlements where a different architectural sensibility developed. We get the same feeling when we visit small towns that still retain their old-style "character." The architectural styles and spatiality—the design of the buildings and the way they are constructed, the size of the streets, the relationships of the buildings to one another, the kinds of businesses you find—all contribute to a refreshing feeling of difference.

There are essentially two ways to find the differences and novelty that tourists seek. One involves space (you go someplace different) and the other involves time (you go back in time). "Old town" experiences involve a kind of time travel because visitors can go back in time, even though in a certain sense, like many tourist experiences, it is artificial. Going into an old-style drug store with a soda fountain and getting an ice-cream soda or frappe is the kind of thing tourists can do when exploring old towns, experiencing a momentary form of cultural regression.

CHANGES IN MUSEUMS

Let me turn to another topic related to how cities market themselves—the changes in museums that have taken place now that they have redefined themselves, to some degree, as tourist destinations and entertainment sites rather than storehouses of "great works of art." Museums can have an enormous impact on a city's identity and image. Think, for example, of architect Frank Gehry's Guggenheim museum in Bilbao. It is generally recognized as a building of international distinction that has put Bilbao on the map and serves as an important tourist attraction.

The same can be said for other cultural institutions, such as the Sydney Opera House, built in 1957, which has become a symbol of Sydney and helped change its image in the minds of tourists. It is also, like museums, a big business, with several thousand performances a year in its four theaters.

Tourists want places to go and things to do when they visit a city, and museums and other elite cultural institutions now must be seen as an increasingly important part of the draw a city has. Internationally distinguished architects are sought out to design museums or their new additions. Museums have also become sites for concerts, films, and other kinds of elite cultural—and more recently, pop cultural—entertainment. Postmodernism has argued that the so-called distinction between elite and popular culture is spurious. This has led many museums to change their sense of mission, so now it is not unusual to see an exhibition of Harley Davidson motorcycles or comic strips in a museum.

Museums and other cultural institutions, then, are shaped to varying degrees by tourism and its imperatives. Urban tourists come to cities for a variety of reasons—conferences, special events (such as carnivals), sporting events, good restaurants, shopping, festive marketplaces, and cultural opportunities. Museums represent one of the main attractions for tourists.

Christopher M. Law writes in his book *Urban Tourism: Attracting Visitors to Large Cities*:

> Large cities are arguably the most important type of tourist destination across the world. They have always attracted visitors but until recently, with the exception of capital cities like London and Paris, the tourist industry has not been perceived as a significant one, nor have these cities been classified as tourist centers. . . . With a large population, facilities such as museums, shops, theatres and sports have been developed to a high standard for local people, and these would have drawn visits from at least the wider region. (1993, 1)

Law adds that around the 1980s things changed and cities decided, for a number of reasons, to develop tourism, which was seen as a growth industry. To stimulate tourism in an increasingly competitive battle for tourists, cities built convention halls, sports stadiums, and museums, often clustering sites to make it easier for tourists to take advantage of them. These amenities, of course, benefited locals and also attracted businesses that were seeking appealing cities for their employees. So museums play an important role in the development of tourism and also enhance the quality of life of a city (or area, since not all museums are in big cities).

There was always something obsessive about Walt Disney's personality. His single-minded concentration on his career, his possessiveness about his business, his unwillingness to share its management with any outsiders, his singular identification with The Mouse, the paternalism and parsimony that marked his dealings with employees—all these qualities now began to be noted as the organization started growing and Disney necessarily grew more remote.

—*Richard Schickel,* The Disney Version

Disneyland, to him [Disney], was a living monument to himself and his ideas of what constituted the good, true and beautiful in this world. It was a projection, on a gigantic scale, of his personality. . . . It was, and is, a statement containing, in general and in particular, conscious expressions of everything that was important to Disney, unconscious expressions of everything that had shaped his personality and of a good many things that had, for good and ill, shaped all of us who are Americans born in this century.

—*Richard Schickel,* The Disney Version

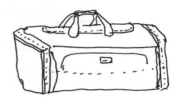

8

Disneyland and Walt Disney World

In this analysis I will discuss Disneyland and Walt Disney World (WDW), certainly among the most famous tourist attractions in the world (now being replicated in a number of other countries) and quintessential representatives, in the eyes of many scholars, of American culture and society.

DISNEYLAND AND WALT DISNEY WORLD

Disneyland and Walt Disney World—and what they reflect about American culture—have long been a subject of fascination for many scholars. Consider the ideas of Jean Baudrillard, who sees Disneyland and its offspring as primary examples of what he calls hyperreality—the dominance of simulations over reality. What follows comes from a translation of Jean Baudrillard's "Disneyworld Company," published on March 4, 1996, in the Parisian newspaper, *Liberation* (the translation is by Francois Debrix):

> Disney, the precursor, the grand initiator of the imaginary as virtual reality, is now in the process of capturing all the real world to integrate it into its synthetic universe, in the form of a vast "reality show" where reality itself becomes a spectacle [*vient se donner en spectacle*], where the real becomes a theme park. The transfusion of the real is like a blood transfusion, except that here it is a transfusion of real blood into the exsanguine universe of virtuality. After the prostitution of the imaginary, here is now the hallucination of the real in its ideal and simplified version.
>
> **At Disney World** in Orlando, they are even building an identical replica of the Los Angeles Disneyland, as a sort of historical attraction to the second degree, a simulacrum to the second power. . . .
>
> **The New World Order** is in a Disney mode. But Disney is not alone in this mode of cannibalistic attraction. We saw Benetton with its commercial campaigns, trying to recuperate the human drama of the news (AIDS, Bosnia,

poverty, apartheid) by transfusing reality into a New Mediatic Figuration (a place where suffering and commiseration end in a mode of interactive resonance). The virtual takes over the real as it appears, and then replicates it without any modification [*le recrache tel quel*], in a *prêt-à-porter* (ready-to-wear) fashion.

What happens, Baudrillard suggests, is that the simulation becomes dominant and replicates the reality it imitates, which then imitates the imitation it has created. Thus, WDW is a simulation of Disneyland, which is a simulation of America. Baudrillard has even argued that now we must consider Disneyland and WDW to be the ultimate reality and America has become an imitation of it!

In his book *Vinyl Leaves: Walt Disney World and America*, S. M. Fjellman adds to this discussion:

> The concepts of real and fake, however, are too blunt to capture the subtlety of Disney simulations. At WDW things are not just real or fake but real real, fake real, real fake, and fake fake. (1992, 255)

So Disneyland and WDW pose difficult problems to people who are interested in the nature of Disney's appeal. Let me offer two analyses that deal with this matter.

A SOCIO-SEMIOTIC ANALYSIS OF DISNEYLAND

The question arises—what makes Disneyland and WDW so popular? One answer to this question comes from Mark Gottdiener, a sociologist who uses semiotics in his analyses of phenomena. He suggests, based on numerous visits to Disneyland, that it offers contemporary urban Americans an experience they desire but cannot experience in modern cities—the experience of growing up in a small town.

This experience is romanticized in our literature and popular culture. Disneyland, he argues, re-creates three mythic small towns—Main Street, New Orleans Square, and Bear Country—and Disneyland's four "realms" also help modern Americans recapture the small-town experience for which they long. Gottdiener also believes that there is a subtext to Disneyland that people who visit it don't recognize—the four realms of Disneyland also can be understood to represent important stages in the development of capitalism.

A PSYCHIATRIST ANALYZES DISNEY AND HIS CREATIONS

Psychiatrist Michael Brody offers a different perspective on Disney's appeal in his fascinating 1975 article (unpublished) "The Wonderful World of Disney—

Its Psychological Appeal." He starts his article with a brief biography of Walt Disney, who was born in Kansas, attended an art school, and then came to California to seek his fortune. Brody discusses a Disney animated film, "The Three Little Pigs," which was made in 1932, and finds it celebrates the virtue of obsessiveness:

> Anal themes are used defensively to lessen the anxiety of oral aggression, represented by the wolf's desire to eat the succulent pigs. Incorporation is certainly a favorite theme in fairy tales and other Disney adventures: the whale swallowing Pinocchio's father; Alice engulfed by the Looking Glass; Captain Hook being chased by the crocodile. There is also the compulsive repetition in the story, going from house to house with the wolf and pigs saying the same phrases. This anality reaches its zenith when the wolf is punished by the huge mechanical spanking machine. (1975, 2–3)

Brody suggests that Disney demonstrated what psychologists describe as anal tendencies. In this regard, Brody mentions Richard Schickel's book on Disney, which noted that he was obsessive, parsimonious, and single-minded and had a need for order—all marks of an anal personality. Disney's anality was reflected in the films he made and, ultimately, in his greatest creation—Disneyworld, an area twice the size of Manhattan island and about the same size as San Francisco.

Brody writes:

> All of the Florida land is under the direct control of the Disney organization, and control, not amusement, seems the central theme in both the California and Florida parks. . . . There is excellent crowd control here. We are led on by the next attraction up the street. Lines may be long, but broken up into smaller units they appear shorter. Employees are young and clean cut. All go to training school for smile and behavior regulation. . . . The overall park environment couldn't be cleaner, or neater and in Florida, even the lakes, forests and beaches are ecologically planned. Waste baskets blend with the scenery and there is even a crew of chewing gum scrapers. Time is also controlled. (1975, 6)

Brody's picture of Disneyland and WDW is that of a psychiatrist who has been trained to look beneath the superficial aspects of people's behavior (and other phenomena, as well) to see what is really going on.

DISNEY'S ANALITY AND ITS CONSEQUENCES

From Brody's perspective, Disneyland is only superficially a self-proclaimed and self-described "happiest place on earth." What he sees is an amusement park in which the anality and obsessiveness of Disney's personality are manifested and disguised. He finds regulation, compartmentalization, and passivity in Disneyland.

One's experience in Disneyland is structured, and there is little to do except spectate. "Except for a penny arcade on Main Street," he writes, "there are no skills to be tested or games to be played. Like being at the movies, you become a receptacle of experiences." Brody believes that Disney's experiences with movies helped him design the park, which is unlike other amusement parks in that it has themes and plots. There is continuity, he explains, in the park's divisions and individual rides, and thus Disneyland provides certain emotional benefits to visitors:

> You enter on Main Street, and your mind begins to gain a new frame of reference. The bricks of the buildings are diminutive in size, in exact ratio to real brick, presenting an illusion of smallness. This entrance is our gateway into the nostalgia of our childhood. Main Street may have existed in Disney's background, but not in most of our real pasts. . . . One may speak of Disney representing the archetypes of our past, and successfully reproducing them in his work. Main Street does bridge our continuity with the past. In a transient society, roots become valued. Here may be our ties, again not in the reality of New York City or Los Angeles, but in the *Saturday Evening Post* with the Rockwell pictures that we absorbed. (1975, 7)

Brody's article helps us understand the appeals of the Disney parks—they enable us to escape from our everyday lives and return to our mythic small-town past. This appeal is similar to our fascination with "old towns" described in chapter 7. But Disneyland and WDW also exert considerable, but subtle, control on us when we visit them, which explains why some critics have described Disney's parks as quasi totalitarian in nature. "Disney," writes Brody, "strove for control over his work and destiny. What could be more natural than a huge, controlled playground where all could be Disney-regulated?" (1975, 6).

People who visit Disneyland and WDW may also feel some kind of comfort, even though they may not be aware of it, in being controlled for a short period of time and having the burden of decision making and choice lifted from their shoulders. This would represent a psychological regression to earlier stages in our development (infancy) when we experienced unconditional love and when strong parental figures were there to look after us. We can see that Disneyland and WDW are considerably more than amusement parks, and their power and appeal continue to interest scholars in many different disciplines.

THE POSTMODERN PERSPECTIVE AND DISNEY

In *Tourism and Modernity*, sociologist Ning Wang offers an insight into how Disneyland, and simulations in general, is regarded by postmodernists:

> Implied in the approaches of postmodernism is justification of the contrived, the copy, and the imitation. One of the most interesting responses to this postmodern cultural condition is Cohen's recent justification of contrived attractions in tourism. According to him, postmodern tourists have become less concerned with the authenticity of the original. . . . Two reasons can be identified. First, if the cultural sanction of the modern tourist has been the "quest for authenticity," then that of the postmodernist tourist is a "playful search for enjoyment" or an "aesthetic enjoyment of surfaces." Secondly, the postmodern tourist becomes more sensitive to the impact of tourism upon fragile host communities or tourist sights. Staged authenticity thus helps project a fragile toured culture and community from disturbance by acting as a substitute for the original and keeping tourists away from it. (2000, 55)

Wang argues that postmodern tourists—by which he means, for the most part, contemporary tourists, since we are living in a postmodern age—are not concerned with authenticity the way modernist tourists were; postmodern tourists are more interested in having fun and thus find "staged" authenticity (or simulations) perfectly acceptable. In addition, as Wang points out, these simulated attractions boast another benefit—they help fragile tourist sites maintain themselves.

Disneyland and WDW remain what might be described as "sites of contestation" in that scholars of different disciplinary and ideological persuasions find many things either to attack or to praise in these parks. Whether you see Disneyland and WDW as the happiest places on earth or as semifascist enclaves, they remain extremely important factors in the growth of world tourism, whose appeals and impact demand consideration by scholars.

Narrative structures have the status of spatial syntaxes. By means of a whole panoply of codes, ordered ways of proceeding and constraints, they regulate changes in space (or moves from one place to another) made by stories in the form of spaces put in linear or interlaced series: from here (Paris), one goes there (Montargis); this place (a room) includes another (a dream or a memory). . . . Every story is a travel story—a spatial practice.

—*Michel de Certeau,* The Practice of Everyday Life

9

The End of the Road

A journey of a thousand miles starts with a step . . . and ends with a step. We have now come to "the end of the road," so to speak, as far as this cultural analysis of tourism is concerned. We have seen that tourism is a very complicated matter that involves and affects many different aspects of our daily lives and our societies, whether we recognize this or not.

Consider museums and the way they have changed because of tourism. We now see that museums play an important role in the "sell" a city has for tourists—the same way that professional baseball, football, basketball, and hockey teams help sell a city as a tourist destination . . . and the same way that beautiful parks, upscale shopping areas, theaters, symphony orchestras, ballets, opera companies, and international class restaurants help sell cities.

GLOBALIZING THE TOURIST GAZE

John Urry, a British sociologist who has done important work on tourism, updates some of his ideas in a recent paper, available on the Internet at www.comp.lancs.ac.uk/sociology/soc079ju.html. His article "Globalising the Tourist Gaze" considers how important globalization has become for tourism. He says that in 1990, when he published his book *The Tourist Gaze*, it was unclear "how significant the processes we now call 'globalisation' were to become." He describes new developments in tourism as follows:

> Significantly for the "tourist gaze" an array of developments are taking "tourism" from the margins of the global order, and indeed of the academy, to almost the centre of this emergent world of "liquid modernity." First, tourism infrastructures have been constructed in what would have been thought of as the unlikeliest of places. . . . Further, there are large increases in the growth of

tourists emanating from very different countries, especially those of the "ori-
ent," that once were places visited and consumed by those *from* the "west." . . .
Moreover, many types of work are now found with these circuits of global
tourism. It is difficult not to be implicated within, or affected by, one or more
of these circuits that increasingly overlap with a more general "economy of
signs" spreading across multiple spaces of consumption (Lash and Urry, 1994).
Such forms of work include transportation, hospitality (including sex tourism:
Clift and Carter, 1999), travel, design and consultancy; the producing of "images" of global tourist sites, of global icons (the Eiffel Tower), iconic types (the
global beach), and vernacular icons (Balinese dances); the mediatizing and cir-
culating of images through print, TV, news, internet and so on; and the organizing through politics and protest campaigns for or against the construction or
development of tourist infrastructures.

Clearly, as Urry points out, there is very little in life, anywhere in the world,
that is not affected either directly or indirectly by the development of global
tourism. It has moved from "the margins" (i.e., from the status of being something of interest but of minor importance) to the center of the world economy. Tourism is now the dominant industry in the world, which probably
explains why it is also becoming a subject of increasing academic interest in
universities everywhere.

TRAVEL AS A MEANS OF WRITING ONE'S LIFE
Michel de Certeau, a distinguished French scholar, suggests in his book *The
Practice of Everyday Life* that stories always involve travel, always involve characters moving from one place to another. "Every story is a travel story" (1984,
115). The fact that there is a spatial dimension to stories leads me to suggest a
hypothesis worth thinking about—that as we move about the world, as we
travel from place to place, we are, in effect, "writing" the stories of our lives.

What I've done with my hypothesis is to take de Certeau's notion and reverse things. If stories always involve travel, then travel always involves stories. And what is the story that our travels tell? Nothing less than some of
the most important moments in our lives! In a curious way, the stories of
our lives become mixed up with our travels and maybe even become our
travels. The periods in between our travels become a kind of inert, shape-
less matter in these stories—filled with the routines and the obligations of
everyday life.

I can recall reading a work by an anthropologist that dealt with headhunting tribes. It seems they spent years planning each headhunting expedition; it became the center of their lives and kept their cultures animated. They had any number of rituals and practices connected with each forthcoming headhunting expedition. When colonial powers prevented these tribes from headhunting, the center of their cultures collapsed. With that collapse, the tribes fell apart and many people died, it seems, because without their rituals and an organizing principle, life was no longer interesting or worth living.

Let me suggest that traveling plays a role something like the ancient headhunting expeditions played for primitive tribes. For the traveler there are guidebooks to get, travel articles and books to read, and all kinds of things to do, including such matters as deciding on the itinerary to take; purchasing cruise, plane, or train tickets; getting required medical inoculations; obtaining visas; booking hotels; finding lists of restaurants to investigate; and booking concert tickets. Even people who take group tours must decide where they want to go, which company to book with, and which, if any, optional city tours to take.

In addition, a good deal of strenuous physical activity is often involved in tourism—including the fact that one often needs to take long and tiring plane trips and generally do a great deal of walking when sightseeing. All of these things become part of our stories and later our memories and the subjects of many conversations. It is because traveling involves "writing" our stories that tourism has such a hold on us. Tourism helps us define ourselves, helps us obtain and consolidate our identities as, through our travels, we "write" the stories of our lives. (Nowadays, with the price of video cameras so low, we often film the stories of our lives, as well.) Portrayals of tourism as just one more form of consumption in a consumption culture are, to my way of thinking, simplistic and grossly inadequate.

SEEING TOURISM FROM ALL SIDES NOW

The cultural studies approach to tourism attempts to look at tourism not from both sides but from all sides, so to speak, to deconstruct the tourism phenomenon and analyze how it affects any number of different areas of contemporary life. Curiously, very few books on tourism take this approach, perhaps because scholars who work in cultural studies have tended to focus their attention on mass mediated culture—that is, on the media and the texts they carry.

I would hope that my attempt to deal with the way the tourism phenomenon informs, permeates, affects, and perhaps even shapes the many different aspects of our society and culture will function as a kind of revelation. I believe that John Urry is correct and that tourism has moved from the margins of society to the economic center of the modern world. It is important, then, that we recognize this fact and its implications. We must start paying more attention to the impact that tourism is having, not only on the society and culture where we live but on all cultures and societies, in every part of the world.

NOTES FROM A 1986 TRAVEL JOURNAL

I've kept journals since 1954, and when I go on a trip I usually take a small notebook along with me to function as a travel journal. In 1986 my wife and I took a trip to China that involved stops, for a few days or so, in Tokyo and later, at the end of our trip, in Taipei. What follows are notes about Japan, our first stop, and about tourism, in general, that I wrote in my journal during the trip. I also include a comic poem I wrote about tourists.

JAPAN (topics to consider)

Miniaturization, hypermodernism, expensive, uniformity, squat toilets, Tokyo isn't Japan, Sumo wrestlers, Japanese aesthetic, alcoholism, stress and pressure, work ethic, sense of place, organization, conscientious, the Ginza, the Palace, the Magi shrine, the tourist office.

* * *

TOURISTS (topics to consider)

Maps, menus, guidebooks, currency conversion charts, seeing sights, cultural treasures, chance encounters with others who speak the same language, dislocation and a lack of "sense" in things, getting lost, walking endlessly, encountering the strange and exotic, unexpected expenses (higher than anticipated but "what the hell"), meeting interesting people and swapping stories about places traveled.

* * *

Alas, the tourist.
He enters a country
the richest,
And leaves it,
The poorest.

* * *

There are lots of people in the airport lounge in all kinds of dress. . . . Most are quite casual. After not doing any international travel for ages—since my trip to Finland six or seven years ago, it is quite exciting. Curious . . . so many people wandering all over the world . . . while most of us spend our lives immersed in the everyday. Where are all these people going?

What's interesting to me is that a number of the themes discussed in this book first manifested themselves in my journal in 1986, some sixteen years before I began this project. And long before reading Barthes's book on Japan, I had noted, though in a more general way, some of the same topics that caught his attention. So, long before I sat down and actually started writing this book, questions about the nature of tourism had occurred to me, and the seeds of the book, so to speak, had begun to form in my mind.

Bibliography

Abram, Simone, Jacqueline Waldren, and Donald V. L. McLeod, eds. 1997. *Tourists and Tourism: Identifying with People and Places.* Oxford, England: Berg.

Adler, Elkan Nathan. 1930. *Jewish Travelers.* London: Routledge.

Armstrong, David. 2001. "Good Morning, Hanoi." *San Francisco Chronicle*, August 5, T1.

Bakhtin, Mikhail. 1984. *Rabelais and His World.* Translated by Helene Iswolsky. Bloomington: Indiana University Press.

Barthes, Roland. 1972. *Mythologies.* New York: Hill and Wang.

———. 1982. *Empire of Signs.* New York: Hill and Wang.

Baudrillard, Jean. 1956. *The System of Objects.* London: Verso.

———. 1996. "Disneyworld Company." *Liberation.* March 4.

———. 1998. *The Consumer Society: Myths and Structures.* London: Sage.

Berger, Arthur Asa, ed. 1989. *Political Culture and Public Opinion.* New Brunswick, N.J.: Transaction.

———. 2004. *Ocean Travel and Cruising: A Cultural Perspective.* Binghamton, N.Y.: Haworth Hospitality Press.

Berger, John. 1972. *Ways of Seeing.* New York: Penguin.

Best, Steven, and Douglas Kellner. 1991. *Postmodern Theory: Critical Interrogations.* New York: Guilford.

Boorstin, Daniel. 1961. *The Image: A Guide To Pseudo-Events in America.* New York: Harper and Row.

Brody, Michael. 1975. "The Wonderful World of Disney—Its Psychological Appeal." Unpublished paper.

Brown, Alan. 2002. "Bangkok Modern." *Travel + Leisure.* October.

Brownmiller, Susan. 1994. *Seeing Vietnam: Encounters of the Road and Heart.* New York: Harper Collins.

Buford, Bill, ed. 1984. *Granta: Travel Writing.* Cambridge, England: Granta.

Camus, Albert. 1963. *Notebooks, 1935–1942.* New York: Knopf.

Certeau, Michel de. 1984. *The Practice of Everyday Life.* Berkeley: University of California Press.

Dickinson, Bob, and Andy Vladimir. 1997. *Selling the Sea: An Inside Look at the Cruise Industry.* New York: Wiley.

Durkheim, Emile. 1965. *The Elementary Forms of Religious Life.* New York: Free Press.

Eliade, Mircea. 1961. *The Sacred and the Profane: The Nature of Religion.* New York: Harper Torchbooks.

Falk, Pasi, and Colin Campbell, eds. 1997. *The Shopping Experience.* London: Sage.

Faulkner, Bill, Gianna Moscardo, and Eric Laws, eds. 2000. *Tourism in the Twenty-First Century: Reflections on Experience.* London: Continuum.

Fjellman, S. M. 1992. *Vinyl Leaves: Walt Disney World and America.* Boulder, Colo.: Westview.

Fussell, Paul, ed. 1987. *The Norton Book of Travel.* New York: Norton.

Goeldner, Charles R., J. R. Brent Richie, and Robert W. McIntosh. 1999. *Tourism: Principles, Practices, Philosophies,* 8th ed. New York: Wiley.

Gottdiener, M. 1995. *Postmodern Semiotics: Material Culture and the Forms of Postmodern Life.* Oxford: Blackwell.

Herodotus. *History of the Persian Wars.* c. 440 B.C.

Iyer, Pico. 1993. *Falling Off the Map: Some Lonely Places of the World.* New York: Knopf.

Law, Christopher M. 1993. *Urban Tourism: Attracting Visitors to Large Cities.* London: Mansell.

———, ed. 1996. *Tourism in Major Cities.* London: Routledge.

Leed, Eric J. 1991. *The Mind of the Traveler: From Gilgamesh to Global Tourism.* New York: Basic Books.

Lévi-Strauss, Claude. 1970. *Tristes Tropiques: An Anthropological Study of Primitive Societies in Brazil.* New York: Atheneum.

Lyotard, Jean-François. 1984. *The Postmodern Condition: A Report on Knowledge.* Minneapolis: University of Minnesota Press.

MacCannell, Dean. 1976. *The Tourist: A New Theory of the Leisure Class.* New York: Schocken.

McLuhan, Marshall. 1965. *Understanding Media: The Extensions of Man.* New York: McGraw-Hill.

Mellencamp, Patricia. 1992. *High Anxiety: Catastrophe, Scandal, Age, & Comedy.* Bloomington: Indiana University Press.

Messaris, Paul. 1997. *Visual Persuasion: The Role of Images in Advertising.* Thousand Oaks, Calif.: Sage.

Milgram, Stanley. 1976. "The Image Freezing Machine." *Society,* November/December: 7–12.

Morris, Jan. 1976. *Travels.* New York: Harcourt Brace Jovanovich.

———. 1980. *Destinations: Essays from Rolling Stone.* New York: Oxford University Press and Rolling Stone.

———. 1984. *Journeys.* New York: Oxford University Press.

———. 1990. *O Canada: Travels in an Unknown Country.* New York: Harper Collins.

Nash, Dennison. 1996. *Anthropology of Tourism.* London: Pergamon.

O'Barr, William M. 1994. *Culture and the Ad: Exploring Otherness in the World of Advertising.* Boulder, Colo.: Westview Press, 1994.

Pearce, Douglas G., and Richard Butler, eds. 1993. *Tourism Research: Critiques and Challenges.* London: Routledge.

Pratt, Mary Louise. 1992. *Imperial Eyes: Travel Writing and Transculturation.* London: Routledge.

Pritchett, V. S. 1989. *At Home and Abroad: Travel Essays by V. S. Pritchett.* San Francisco: North Point Press.

Saussure, Ferdinand de. 1966. *A Course in General Linguistics.* New York: McGraw-Hill.

Schickel, Richard. 1971. *The Disney Version.* New York: Avon Books.

Simmel, Georg. 1997. "The Adventure." In David Frisby and Mike Featherstone (eds.), *Simmel on Culture.* London: Sage.

Theroux, Paul. 1975. *The Great Railway Bazaar.* London: Hamish Hamilton.

———. 1990. *To the Ends of the Earth: The Selected Travels of Paul Theroux.* New York: Random House.

Thubron, Colin. 1999. *In Siberia.* New York: Harper Collins.

Tocqueville, Alexis de. 1956. *Democracy in America.* New York: Mentor.

Turner, Victor. 1974. *Dramas, Fields and Metaphors: Symbolic Action in Human Society.* Ithaca, N.Y.: Cornell University Press.

Urry, John. 2001. "Globalising the Tourist Gaze." Published by the Department of Sociology, Lancaster University. Available: www.comp.lancs.ac.uk/sociology/soc079ju.html [Oct. 15, 2003].

Wang, Ning. 2000. *Tourism and Modernity: A Sociological Analysis.* Oxford, England: Pergamon.

Zeman, J. Jay. 1977. "Peirce's Theory in Signs." In Thomas A. Sebeok (ed.), *A Perfusion of Signs.* Bloomington: Indiana University Press.

Index

About the Author

Arthur Asa Berger is professor emeritus of Broadcast and Electronic Communication Arts at San Francisco State University, where he taught between 1965 until 2003. He graduated in 1954 from the University of Massachusetts, where he majored in literature and philosophy. He received an MA degree in journalism and creative writing from the University of Iowa in 1956. He was drafted shortly after graduating from Iowa and served in the U.S. Army in the Military District of Washington in Washington, D.C., where he was a feature writer and speech writer in the District's Public Information Office. He also wrote high school sports for *The Washington Post* on weekend evenings.

Berger spent a year touring Europe after he got out of the army and then went to the University of Minnesota, where he received a PhD in American Studies in 1965. He wrote his dissertation on the comic strip *Li'l Abner.* In 1963–1964, he had a Fulbright to Italy and taught at the University of Milan. In 1973 he lived in London, where he investigated British popular culture. He also spent a year as visiting professor at the Annenberg School for Communication at the University of Southern California in Los Angeles in 1984.

The author of numerous articles, book reviews, and books on the mass me-
dia, popular culture, humor, and everyday life, Berger's recent books include
*Ocean Travel and Cruising: A Cultural Analysis; The Portable Postmodernist; Ads,
Fads and Consumer Culture;* and *Media & Society.* He has also written a number
of mysteries: *The Hamlet Case; Postmortem for a Postmodernist; The Mass Comm
Murders: Five Media Theorists Self-Destruct;* and *Durkheim Is Dead: Sherlock
Holmes Is Introduced to Sociological Theory.* His books have been translated into
German, Swedish, Italian, Korean, Turkish, Indonesian, and Chinese, and he has
lectured in more than a dozen countries in the course of his career.

Berger is married, has two children and two grandchildren, and lives in Mill
Valley, California. He enjoys traveling and dining in ethnic restaurants. Arthur
Asa Berger can be reached by e-mail at aberger@sfsu.edu or arthurasaberger@
yahoo.com.